Chariot of Knowledge

The Lost History of the Ancient Olympic Games

Sandra Rato

with

Ivo Rato

Contact the author:
http://hourigan.co/authors/rato

ISBNs
978-0-9945943-0-3 (pbk)
978-0-9945943-1-0 (e-book)

Set in Linux Libertine

This book is dedicated not only to those who love history, but above all to the millions of Celts who have been dispersed around the globe.

About the authors

Sandra Rato and her father Ivo Rato worked together in the research and writing of *Chariot of Knowledge: The Lost History of the Ancient Olympic Games*. Their investigation of the Ancient Olympics' secret history is grounded in their Lusitanian (Portuguese Celtic) heritage, and was refined through Sandra's studies in archaeology and anthropology at La Trobe University. Their shared journey towards publishing this book began with a re-enactment of the ancient Isthmian Games in Melbourne in 1990, paying homage to Greek culture while shining light on the games' connection with Celtic sporting traditions.

To contact the authors, please visit *hourigan.co/authors/rato*.

Contents

Foreword

Many Australians have Celtic ancestry: therefore, I endeavour to impart my knowledge of the most important games of ancient Europe—the Celtic Games. This book, which I like to refer to as "The Chariot of Knowledge," has as its aim to remedy the cultural crime committed by ecclesiastical academics against Celtic culture and history. In doing so, it will throw some intellectual light on the sacred truth, which is that the ancient games are connected to the Bible and that famous rituals related to cultural and sporting events were not only Greek but universal practices.

This book collects information, based on ancient records, that comes to us through Greek and Roman historians who witnessed the games. There are indeed a few contemporary authors who have published books based on the ancient games of Greece, but they all tell the same story—that the Greeks competed in what are claimed to be the original games. Surrounding this claim are seven remarkable curiosities (and we shall hear about them soon), which raise what I call the *seven sacramental Olympic questions* (see p.13). Not one of the authors concerned has managed to answer these questions, which led me to begin my investigation.

Thanks to the "Temple of Knowledge," as my father likes to call the Victorian State Library, I found that my questions about the sacramental nature of the Olympics pointed towards parallels with the Old Testament. These remarkable coincidences provide evidence that the scriptures may have been the world's first act of plagiarism. In fact, by looking at the Olympics as an allegory of biblical myths shows that the Greeks, Romans, and Celts must all have known the contents of these scriptures long before the Hebrews wrote their Bible. Not only written research, but also the science of archaeology, brings out this truth. Thanks to the hard work and ingenuity of archaeologists, who have discovered and deciphered precious historical evidence, we are today able to present a story based on facts laid out in written historical accounts.

Archaeology uncovers the truth, rather than serving the interest of any particular religion or political movement. History is not only a matter of time, but also a matter of truth. This book, the Chariot of Knowledge, arrives at an opportune time to share knowledge that historians have not yet been able to teach us.

I have worked closely with my father, Ivo Rato, in preparing this book. In so doing, I have drawn on my background in archaeology and anthropology, while constantly asking the questions that animate this book. While taking a great interest in my father's connection to his Celtic heritage—which is at the centre of this work—I have also delved into issues regarding women and equal rights.

Women were never a part of the Ancient Olympic Games, in the sense that they could not physically compete nor even, with the exception of the priestess of Demeter, be present at them. The only way they could participate was as owners of the horses and chariots used in the competition, and even then they could not with their own eyes witness how their property fared in the games.

Why was this? Perhaps the best way to understand this is by comparing the dogmatic authoritarianism of the Old Testament with the democratic nature of ancient Celtic society. The games were based on the Old Testament, which is why I like to refer to the Ancient Olympics as the Biblical Games. Briefly here—for this is a topic that we will expand upon—Christianity follows the scriptures of the Old Testament and still continues the punishing practice of transforming women into second-class citizens. But the Celtic mentality associated the source of life with both women and men, in contrast to the later doctrines of the Catholic Church, which teaches that women are inferior.

The stories of Pandora and of Adam and Eve paint women as the cause of all the world's iniquities: and history keeps repeating itself, as women continue to pay for this supposed crime. Just recently in the news, we heard the horrible stories of female police officers being sexually harassed by currently serving senior officers.[1] How has this managed to go on for so long? Why are women continually punished? In short, the answer is a lack of education. By contrast with the Christian tradition, Celtic culture taught that women were warriors, fighters, and lovers—strong, and equal to men. With so much Celtic heritage in Australia, women should feel empowered.

This Chariot of Knowledge also raises the topic of paedophilia, another present-day issue whose history reaches back

---

[1]Keith Moor, Lauren Wood, and Kara Irving, "Sexual Harassment within Victoria Police Could Cost Millions with Almost 1000 Alleged Victims," *Herald Sun*, 9 December 2015, http://www.heraldsun.com.au/news/law-order/sexual-harassment-within-victoria-police-could-cost-millions-with-almost-1000-alleged-victims/news-story/8468cb29059d7e4e0a2a c629a2388a93.

5,000 years and that persists in the Catholic Church, which while condemning homosexuality has given shelter to those perpetrating evil acts of paedophilia. I raise this issue for homosexuality, which should not be condemned, dates back to the bi-sexual legacy of the Ancient Olympics. These games were held in honour of Zeus, the father of the gods, who loved young men at the same time as he also had many female lovers.

I want everyone to come along on this journey with me and share the mystical connection my father and I have with our Celtic heritage. My involvement in the Chariot of Knowledge, this lost history of the Ancient Games, inspired me to deepen my interest in archaeology and anthropology under the guidance of my father, Ivo Rato.

An incredible historian, he has provided me with a wealth of knowledge. Our journey to telling this story all began when I witnessed and took part in remaking the Isthmian Games in Melbourne in 1990. My father, the organiser, aimed to educate people by paying homage to and shining light on both Greek and Celtic culture. This year, as we await the 2016 games while the world continues to struggle with unfortunate issues regarding paedophilia and the status of women, presents the perfect time to learn about and contemplate what the secret history of the Ancient Olympic Games can teach us. Let's make 2016 the year of the "Chariot of Knowledge."

Let no one suppose that I am insensible to the merits of Grecian culture. To write about the ancient European festivals, we must be not only poetic but impartial. I am Luso-Australiana—a term I will explain later. My father is Portuguese Celtic or Lusitano in his heart, though he speaks a Latin language, Portuguese, rather than a Celtic language due to the long-ago Romanisation of Lusitania. He is proud to have been born of ancient Celtic Heritage in Lisboa (Lisbon), which at one time in history was named Olissipo, after the legendary Odysseus, known as Ulysses in Latin.

The reciprocal dealings of Greeks and Lusitanos since 600 BC developed intermingled relationships based on commerce and marriage. This mixed heritage inspired my father's passion for Greek history from an early age. His belief is that it was the power of fate, proceeding from celestial bodies and operating on the affairs of men, that gave him the inspiration to pay homage to Grecian culture in that momentous recreation of the Isthmian Games on 18 October 1996. After more than two thousand years since the last of the original Isthmian Games, we saw again the torch race, the Isthmian fire, the throwing of the discus, and even a recreation of the ancient chariot race. That evening, an Olissipo and Isthmian night was held to show Australians the other games of the Olympic Golden Circuit (see p.48), and simultaneously to present my father's devout affection for the Grecian world and shine light on these two great cultures of ancient Europe: the Greek and the Celtic.

To accommodate our guests with a mystical environment appropriate to the occasion, my father erected a huge marquee in a park, furnished it with chairs and tables, and created a warm atmosphere with open fires. Dinner was served by candlelight, to the accompaniment of songs of Dionysus, *fado* or *rembetika*. According to the traditions of the ancient Greek temples of Corinth, we also witnessed the ritual of belly dancing.

Despite modest surroundings, these flourishes, along with the presence of important personalities, good friends, and crowds of people from the community, infused the evening with magic. The night was attended by a martial arts celebrity,

Bob Jones, and other members of his organisation, representatives of the Victorian minister of education, SBS TV, the Portuguese ambassador to Australia and consul for Victoria. The consul general of Greece, George Veis, who is also a philosopher, exalted our work and idea, praising the solemn occasion and the intermingling of the cultures of Greece and Olissipo.

That night marked the beginning of eight years of research in collaboration with my father, culminating in the book you hold in your hands: *Chariot of Knowledge: The Lost History of the Ancient Olympic Games.*

Sandra Rato
10 June 2016

1. The Chariot of Knowledge

From the time of sacred religion to the time of the sacred dollar.

After a journey of more than five thousand years, finally it arrives: the Chariot of Knowledge. We carry the torch to illuminate the sacred truth and establish the connection between the Ancient Olympic Games and the Bible. Until now it has been a secret known only to a few that the games were designed according to biblical correspondences that are surrounded by mystery and intrigue.

Humans delight in mystery, which is beyond reason. The Chariot of Knowledge discloses meanings hidden since the time of the biblical flood told of in the Old Testament, and also secrets relating to the Virgin Mary, Mary Magdalene, and the Passion of Christ—all from the New Testament. Based on today's archaeological evidence, we are now able to disclose to you phenomena that have been wrapped in mystery for thousands of years.

This Chariot of Knowledge carries not only five thousand years of written history, but also treats of the puzzling events surrounding the fabled city of Atlantis—the lost paradise of Plato. Here you will see that the sacred rituals of Atlantis are being practiced even now, in a few parts of the world, giving the traditions of which we speak a remote heredity of more than ten thousand years.

To many readers, this may seem like a long time in human history. But as we continue to make new discoveries, we may one day finally realise that the history of civilisation is far longer than the history books commonly tell us.

Mankind loves the past. Whether prosperous or adverse events have marked the course of our lives, we wish not only that *we* should remember them, but that our children should remember them, and their children's children. It is Providence that has planted in the human mind this desire, which is among those things that elevate humans above the brute. This desire is intimately connected with the awareness that we do not stand alone but belong to a society, and not only to the past, but to the future.

The art of writing, especially in the simple Roman alphabet that the languages of Europe have spread across the world, has perhaps done more for the improvement of the human race than any other invention. Like other great blessings, it has been attended by some evils—such as the use of biblical scriptures to teach that women are responsible for all mankind's iniquities—but it has also been the most efficient means of raising mankind from barbarism to civilisation. Without the aid of writing, the experience of each generation would have been almost entirely lost to succeeding ages, and we would today only discern a faint glimmer of the truth of the past through the mist of tradition.

The science of archaeology: A matter of truth

Thanks to the capacity of ancient civilisations to preserve their ideas for posterity, in combination with the hard work and ingenuity of archaeologists who have discovered and deciphered precious historical evidence, today we can present a story based on the facts of written history and the archaeological record, which serves not the interest of any religion or political movement, but only the truth.

Because history is not only a matter of time but also a matter of the truth, we can be thankful that the Chariot of Knowledge has arrived, carrying the side of the story of the past that historians have, to date, forgotten or neglected to tell us.

The Ancient Olympic Games

Few other sporting or cultural events on earth are as capable of capturing the world's attention as the modern Olympics. This gives us a clear reason for bringing further light to the history of their predecessor—the Ancient Olympic Games. Millions of sports fans around the world deserve not just this book, but a far deeper body of scholarship on the subject. Those who love the modern event will doubtlessly want to know how the ancient Greeks organised their festivals: how they competed, what events they had, how the athletes were selected, how they timed the results, and above all, why they created the games in the first place.

In other words: the world will want to know the original meaning behind the sacred Ancient Olympic Games.

There are always two sides to every story, and the Ancient Olympic Games present no exception to this rule. Like the biblical "chariot of fire," the Chariot of Knowledge carries enough light to illuminate the other side of history. Since the truth has not suited religious and political purposes, ecclesiastical academics have decided to keep it in the dark. This book will present the evidence and give you the chance to make up your own mind.

2. Destiny: The Corinthian Temple of Melbourne

The Temple of Knowledge—The State Library of Victoria

We will always be grateful to Australia for the gift of understanding Celtic culture. Here, in the State Library of Victoria, we found works that awakened a sixth sense, the faculty by which we perceive the vital powers of the cosmos and the knowledge they have to impart. By "cosmic laws," we mean mysteries incomprehensible to human intelligence.

The sixth sense and cosmic communication

As soon as they began to observe the world around them, men and women could not help seeing the close connection between themselves and external nature. When the sun sets, humans want rest. Atmospheric changes affect our health, and wounds can become painful with a change in the weather or at certain phases of the moon. Some people are affected by the presence of particular animals, while certain liquids exhilarate and others destroy life.

From an early age, I have felt excitement and spiritual affection at the thought of the sacred history of my ancestors, and of the heroes who take part in it. Wanting to know the history of my ancestors sparked many confrontations with my teachers. Sometimes they refused to answer questions because they didn't know the answers; at other times they refused—or were ignorant of the truth—because of their political and religious interests. But without reading any book or talking to any professor, I knew three things about my ancestors: they had a very sophisticated type of self-defence, they had strong religious beliefs, and they had a kind of Olympic Games.

The Australian connection to our Celtic lineage

I had an intense desire to discover the meaning of the Ancient Olympic Games, and the ambition awakened in my mind drove me to make amazing discoveries. Since such a large proportion of the Australian population is of Celtic ancestry, I am now making an attempt to impart what I have learned about the most important games of Ancient Europe: the Celtic Games. The objective of this book—the Chariot of Knowledge—is to overcome the cultural crime that ecclesiastical academics have committed against my people, the Celts, and throw intellectual light on the sacred truth.

The Ancient Games were connected to the Bible, and therefore, the ancient rituals of these cultural and sporting events were not only Greek practices but universal ones. This book collects information based on ancient records that come to us via Greek and Roman historians who were eyewitnesses to the games, and because of their central place in world history, I'm lucky not to have needed to know ancient Greek or Latin to read them: Aristotle, Socrates, the poet Pindar, the historians Herodotus, Strabo, Pausanias, and many others, all of which saw the games in person. Fortunately, their work is still available, after so many years, for us to investigate—and historians such as ourselves, who don't understand the ancient Greek or Celtic languages, are grateful for the work of those who translated the old documents for us to investigate.

Few contemporary authors write about the ancient games of Greece. Some are more accurate than others, but they all tell of how the Greeks competed in the original games. And they all mention seven remarkable curiosities, which pose tantalising questions—to which no author has yet delivered the answers. These are the seven sacramental Olympic questions (from now on, "the seven questions"), and in this book *we* will answer them.

The seven sacramental Olympic questions

1. Why were the victors in the Olympics crowned with garlands of olive leaves, when all authors on the subject explain that the games were dedicated to Zeus, the father of the gods, whose sacred tree was the oak?

2. Why did the wrestling contests take place around the altar of Zeus, and not in the stadium along with the rest of the sports, and why did they have no time limit?

3. Why were the Olympiads for a long time named after the victors, runners of the stadion?

13

4. Why did the ancient games of Europe all originate as funeral games?

5. What did the torch relay race mean?

6. Why was a sacred truce, the *hieromenia*, strictly imposed?

7. Why were women not allowed to compete in the Olympics?

Believing the games must have been designed for a specific purpose, I started to investigate, hoping to find their meaning. Thanks to the "Temple of Knowledge," aka the Victorian State Library, I gradually found sources directing me to the conclusion that the seven questions all related to a relationship between the games and the scriptures of the Old Testament. And this, in turn, revealed that these scriptures are the first historically noteworthy act of plagiarism in the world. In fact, by seeing that the Olympics were an allegory of biblical myths, once can realise that the Greeks, Romans, and Celts all knew the contents of these scriptures long before the Hebrews wrote their Bible.

3. The mythical origins of the Ancient Olympic Games

There are many opinions on the mythological origin of the games.

According to one story, Zeus founded the games after his victory over the Titans. During these games, Mars won the prize in boxing and Apollo outran mercury in a foot race. Others credited the games to the Argonauts, and in another myth, Pelops founded the games in honour of Zeus. Even Heracles has been named the founder of the Olympics, which he dedicated to Zeus.

According to Sir James Frazer, the famous Celtic anthropologist,[1] the Olympic Games have their origins in the Greek doctrine of rebirth and the rites of the sacrificial killing of kings. Frazer is regarded as one of the founders of modern anthropology, and his famous, multivolume work, *The Golden Bough*, published between 1890 and 1915, traces the development of world religions from their earliest forms. Frazer taught social anthropology at the universities of Liverpool and Cambridge, and published many other works, including *Totemism and Exogamy* and *Folklore in the Old Testament*.

Being a great connoisseur of Greek culture, Frazer also published translations of Pausanias, and once said that without

---

[1]Born Glasgow, Scotland, 1 Jan 1854; died 7 March 1941.

Pausanias, the history of Greece would be a labyrinth without a clue. From our perspective, without Frazer's work, the history of the Ancient Games would be riddled with secrets kept only by God, and so I strongly recommend that readers in search of the deepest understanding of the rituals of the Ancient Games should also consult *The Golden Bough.*

I became acquainted with Frazer's work through my father, and *he* encountered him, remarkably, through what he calls "cosmic communication". There are two ways to consult a library. First, after carefully organising our documentation, we may ask a librarian to guide us according to our needs. Second, the method that my father prefers—one may browse along the bookshelves and try to sense the vibes of the authors who have their works displayed there, allowing the books to entice one into picking them up.

4. Mythology

A nation's mythology consists of the whole body of its traditions regarding its gods and heroes. In the West, when we hear the word *mythology* we most often think of the Greeks and Romans, because for a long time these were the mythoi most commonly investigated. But lately, attention has also been paid to the mythologies of other peoples: the Celts, Hindus, Native Americans, Chinese, Sumerians, and so on.

We may regard myths and fables as mainly the invention of crafty priests; allegorical expositions of the truth; gross conceptions of the divine, formed by the ignorant; or historical facts varied and exaggerated by tradition, embellished by poetry and purposefully altered by cunning. Whichever of these views we take, myths will always retain their interest for the historian, who, in their search for truth, finds it as important to study mankind's fancies and fabrications as to study its plainspoken truths.

Mythology from the beginning of the twentieth century

When my father was a little child, there was no television, so one of his favourite pastimes was to indulge in evening parties and enjoy listening to his grandfather, a sailor, tell stories of his past travels. His grandmother also had interesting stories to tell, and one of these fits the story of mythology from the beginning of the twentieth century.

At the beginning of the twentieth century, my father's grandmother was a little girl living in Estarreja–Ovar, an area near the coast in the north of Portugal. One day, the villagers were disturbed by "a moving wagon without horses." The people went on their knees, put their hands together, and prayed for salvation. The cause of this disturbance was, of course, a motor car. The peasants did see a wagon move without the aid of horses, and because they could not understand modern technology, they blamed it on the Devil.

This episode shows how mythologies come into being on account of people's ignorance of the causes of natural phenomena. Only a critical analysis can enable us to fully understand the nature and origins of the mythological fables, and also to discern their true meaning within their tangle of symbolic expressions and distorted representations.

Mythology after the Second World War

A few years ago, while watching a television documentary about an Australian expedition to New Guinea, I noticed another example of living mythology from just half a century ago. Members of a New Guinean tribe in the early stages of civilisation, speaking symbolically and out of ignorance, gave the following account of their first meeting with white men. On seeing them for the first time, the tribespeople were scared and believed the men had come to eat them, but when they saw food drop from the sky not long after, they changed their minds and decided that white people were gods. Later, when they saw white men getting into and out of their four-wheel drive cars, they thought these strangers were very lucky because their mother—the car—carried them everywhere.

This is another example of mythology, evidently more primitive than the Portuguese people's reaction to the motor car at the beginning of the twentieth century. Even after the Second World War, this primitive tribe still could not draw the essential connection between a wagon and a motor car, and confused the foreigners' Land Rover with a mother to gods. This perception makes one wonder, when considering such a mythology: could the gods—including *our* gods—have been astronauts?

5. The games of ancient Europe

The world mistakenly believes these five myths (along with many others):

I. History schoolbooks tell us the truth.

II. The Ancient Olympic Games were a Greek creation.

III. At that time, in the eighth century BC, only the Greeks had the capacity to organise such sophisticated cultural, religious, and sporting events.

IV. The Jews created the Bible.

V. The International Olympic Committee is a democratic organisation.

The lost history of the Ancient Olympic Games

Capulugolympia—The triad of religious, cultural, and sporting events of ancient Europe. The Olympic connection with the Bible. Capitoline–Lughnasadh–Olympics.

This is the story of the important religious, cultural, and sporting events of ancient Europe, based on the authors' research into the records laid down by ancient authors—both famous and anonymous—as well as by contemporary writers.

In this work, we owe a debt to the State Library of Victoria, which has fortunately been saved from the destructive efforts of the pious. Without the efforts and intellect of the first settlers, many of them highly educated people convicted of political offences, who built and furnished this Victorian "Temple of Knowledge" with its valuable contents, many of them unique in the world, we would not have been able to find many missing pages that elsewhere had been burned by the zeal of the Catholic Inquisition.

During the time my father was editing a martial arts magazine, searching for articles on ancient combat sports, he first found the answers to some of these questions about the missing details in the story of our Celtic ancestors and their cultures. These books, which in his home country had been burned by the Portuguese Inquisition, were some of the crucial pieces of the puzzle which, when assembled, finally formed the vision of the ancient games that we present here.

One of the most startling aspects of that vision is that *the Greeks were not the creators of the Ancient Olympic Games. Olympic* is of course a word of Greek derivation: it refers to anything regarding the twelve Greek gods dwelling on Mt Olympus, the magnificent residence presided over by omnipotent Zeus. But, as we will demonstrate, the meaning behind the festival of the Ancient Olympic Games was based on the sacred scriptures of the Old Testament—the Greeks took the concept from the authors of the Bible. And at the same time, our research also reveals that the Jews were not the creators of the biblical story, but rather drew on the ideas from another culture—the Babylonians.

The following paragraphs will give an insight to how many ancient civilisations in fact knew the contents of the Old Testament before it was produced and the reason why the Greek games were not the most important games of ancient Europe.

The Greek games were not Europe's most important

Only Greeks could compete in the Olympics, making the games in a certain sense irrelevant to the rest of Europe, and yet the sacred rituals behind the games were extended to other cultures, so that we find elements of the festival are common to other civilisations—and this common tradition is the greater and more important one. Using a contemporary analogy, we might ask whether the Greek national soccer competition is more important than the European Cup. The same situation applies to the ancient games.

The Romans and the Celts also had equivalents to the Ancient Olympics but called them by different names. As the Greek god Zeus was deemed to supervise the Olympics from Mt Olympus, so Jupiter judged the Roman games—the Capitoline Games—from his throne on the Capitoline Hill.

The Roman Capitol

The Roman Capitol has been described thus:

> The Capitol or Citadel of ancient Rome stood on the Capitoline hill, the smallest of the seven hills of Rome, called the Saturnine and Tarpeian rock. It was begun B.C. 614, by Tarquinius Priscus, but was not completed till after the expulsion of the kings. After being thrice destroyed by fire and civil commotion, it was rebuilt by Domitian, who instituted there the Capitoline games. Dionysius says the temple, with the exterior palaces, was 200 feet long, and 185 broad. The whole building consisted of three temples, which were dedicated to Jupiter, Juno, and Minerva, and separated from one another by walls. In the wide portico, triumphal banquets were given to the people. The statue of Jupiter, in the Capitol, represented the god sitting on a throne of ivory and gold, and consisted in the earliest times of clay painted red; under Trajan, it was formed of gold. The roof of the temple was made of bronze; it was gilded by Q. Catulus. The doors were of the same metal. Splendor and expense were profusely lavished upon the whole edifice. The gilding alone cost 12,000 talents (about $12,000,000), for which reason the Romans called it the Golden Capitol. On the pediment stood a chariot drawn by four horses, at first of clay, and afterwards of brass gilded. The temple itself contained an immense quantity of the most magnificent presents. The most important state papers, and particularly the Sibylline books were preserved in it. A few pillars and some ruins are all that now remain of the magnificent temple of Jupiter Capitolinus. Its site is mostly occupied by

the church of the Franciscans, and partly by the modern capitol called theCampidoglio, which was erected after the design of Michael Angelo, consisting of three buildings. From the summit of the middle one, the spectator has a splendid view of one of the most remarkable regions in the world—the Campagna, up to the mountains.[1]

The museums of the Campidoglio contain some of the finest collections of statues and paintings in the world, and the stairs leading up to the equestrian statue of Marcus Aurelius are exceptionally beautiful. Invoking the Campidoglio's grandeur, Thomas Jefferson gave the name "Capitol Hill" to the seat of the United States Congress in Washington.

The Capitoline Games

The passion of the Roman people for the Capitoline Games appears in the cry with which they addressed their rulers—*panem e circenses* (bread and games). A splendid procession, *orpompa*, opened the festival, in which images of the great gods were carried to the temple of Jupiter on the Capitoline Hill. The procession, led by the chief magistrate, moved through this temple, through the forum and the street called Velabrum, to the *Circus Maximus*. Before the magistrate was carried the image of the winged goddess of fortune, *Fortuna Alata*. Then came the images of Jupiter, Juno, Minerva, Neptune, Ceres, Apollo, and

---

[1]S. Spooner, "Anecdotes of Painters, Engravers, Sculptors and Architects and Curiosities of Art," http://grandearte.net/anecdotes-painters-engravers-sculptors-and-architects-and-curiosities-art/anecdotes-painters-engrave, accessed 1 May 2016.

Diana. After the death of Julius Caesar, his image was introduced to the procession, and in later times, perhaps, also those of the deified emperors. These images were carried in splendid, horse-drawn chariots, followed by a parade of stags, camels, elephants, and sometimes lions, panthers, or tigers.

After the pomp-filled procession of gods followed rows of boys who had lost their father or mother, leading the horses to be used in the races. Then came those sons of the patricians who were from fifteen to sixteen years of age, some of them on horseback, and some of them on foot. Following them were the magistrates of the city and the Senate, and then the sons of knights, on horseback and on foot, brought up the rear of the main procession. After it came the chariots and horses destined for the races, and all the different classes of athletes—pugilists, wrestlers, and runners, all naked except for a covering about their loins.

The procession also included dancers, youths and boys arranged in rows according to their age, who wore violet-coloured garments with brass belts, and carried swords and short spears. The men wore helmets, and each division of dancers was preceded by a man who led them. Musicians followed the dancers, including a number of people dressed like satyrs (men with horse- or goat-like features), who with large wreaths of flowers in their hands performed sportive dances, with a company of musicians behind them.

This exhibition of wild, unrestrained joy was followed by more religious pomp. First came the *camilli*, boys who assisted the priests in their sacrifices, and then the servants who also took part in the sacrifices; then the haruspices with their knives, who performed divination by inspecting the sacrificed animals' entrails; and the butchers who led the victims to the altars. Next, there were the different orders of priests and their servants: first the high priest, or *Pontifex Maximus*, the other pontifices, the *flamines* and the augurs, the *quindecimviri* with the Sybilline books, the Vestal Virgins, and then the remaining inferior orders of priests, according to their rank. Further images of the gods brought up the rear, and sometimes there was also a theatrical show of treasures and spoils of war.

In the Circus, the procession went around once in a circle and then the sacrifices were performed. The spectators took their places, the music struck up, and the games began.

First, there were the races with horses and chariots. These were honourable events, and only men of the highest rank engaged in them. The chariots were very light, and commonly had two or four horses attached to them abreast.

Second were the gymnastic contests. Third came the Trojan games: prize contests on horseback, which were said to have been instituted by Aeneas, and which were revived by Julius Caesar. Fourth were the combats with wild beasts, in which animals fought with each other or with men—criminals, slaves, prisoners of war, or volunteers. Fifth and finally came the representations of naval engagements (*naumachiae*), for which the Circus could be put underwater.

These games were phenomenally extravagant and correspondingly expensive: in his second consulship, Pompey brought forward five hundred lions for one combat of wild beasts, and eighteen elephants were slain in five days.[2]

The ritual purpose of the games originated from the same point as their name.

---

[2] "The British Encyclopedia Vol III," http://www.archive.org/stream/bri tishencyclope030478mbp/britishencyclope030478mb (accessed May 01, 2016).

The meaning of the Capitoline Games

The temples of the Capitol were dedicated not only to Jupiter but also to Juno and Minerva, who made up a triad of deities. According to the historian Livy, the cult of Juno was brought to Rome by the Etruscans from the city of Veii in the year 396 BC.

In 378 BC, after the Celts departed Rome, having ransacked the city but failed to take the temple of Jupiter, the statesman and soldier Marcus Furius Camillus dedicated an ancient festival, probably of Etruscan origin, to Jupiter, since the Romans believed that it was he who had prevented the Celts from conquering the temple. Here it is that our story first features the Celts, who dominated Europe long before its Romanisation.

Then, in 86 AD, the emperor Domitian reconstructed the Capitol in great splendour and restored the Capitoline Games to a quinquennial cycle.

At this point, the key thing to note is that the Capitoline Games centred around a funeral festival, a triad of deities, and a quinquennial cycle. These are three essential elements that we see repeated in similar ritual sporting events across the European continent, and this pattern is one important clue that will lead us to the games' true origin.

The Lughnasadh Games

The Celtic god Lugh is said to have arranged the games of the Lughnasadh festival at Tailtiu (now Teltown, in County Meath) at the grave of his foster mother, who gives the place its name. In other versions of the story, Lugh held the games at Tara, in honour of his wives. St Patrick mentions Tara as "*Caput*

Scotorwn", from the Latin *caput* (head) and *Scot*, the ancient name for the Irish.

The Lughnasadh ritual involved three types of sacrifices, as three is the lucky number of the Celts. These were dedicated to the three spirits of vegetation, representing the phases of creation: birth, life, and death. As a quinquennial festival introduced along with an adjustment of the calendar, Lughnasadh reinforced the annual ritual of giving thanks for fertility.

Once again the reader can observe a pattern familiar from the Capitoline Games: the Lughnasadh games were funeral games, involved rituals venerating a triad, and took place according to a quinquennial cycle, also known as a *lustre*. Originating from the root *lu* or *luz*, meaning "light", a lustre is a five-year calendar cycle, and also a chandelier of five branches. Lughnasadh can be considered the quinquennial cycle of Lugh, similar to the Greek Olympic *pentaeteris* (see p.48). A lustral sacrifice was common to the three most important ritual sporting events of ancient Europe, of which the Ancient Olympic Games are today the best-known.

6. The Olympic Games

According to some, Pelops founded the Olympics in honour of his father-in-law, King Oenomaus of Pisa in the Peloponnesus, who lost his life in a legendary chariot race against Pelops. Others say that Heracles started the games when proceeding from Crete to Elis with his brothers Paeoneus, Ida, Jasius, and Epidemes. The four younger brothers contended with each other for a prize in racing, and Heracles (known more often by his Roman name, Hercules) crowned the victor with a wreath of olives taken from a particularly beautiful tree that had been transplanted from the land of Hyperborea to the holy plain near Pisa. Later, this tree alone was used to make the victors' wreaths for the Ancient Olympics.

The Nemean Games, in some accounts, were also established by Heracles, who after his death, was offered a sacrifice of a bull, a wild boar, and a goat by the Argonaut Menoetius, the son of Actor. And the interval between the Ancient Olympic Games was a Greek *pentaeteris*, which slightly exceeded four years. Like the Capitoline Games and the Lughnasadh games, the Ancient Olympics follow the pattern of a funeral games, triad sacrifice, and a quinquennial period.

Suovetaurilia: A trinity sacrifice,
suino–ovinus–taurus

Sacrificium lustrale. A sacrifice of purification, a propitiary offering. *Lustralis* relating to redemption from guilt or the appeasing of the gods. *Lustral*—of the sun and the moon. An expiatory sacrifice every quinquennial cycle, to ensure fertility.

Suino. Swine. Same root as *sow*.

Ovinus. Ovine, from *ovis*, a sheep.

Taurus. Bull. In Portuguese, *touro*.

The sacred triad sacrifice is a common feature of all the most important ritual games that were held in ancient Europe. According to James Frazer, the Ancient Olympic Games were not a harvest festival but were based on astronomical considerations. Whatever one may think of these speculations, the great Olympic festival cannot have been, like the Lammas festival celebrated in England and Scotland, a festival of the harvest, due to the quinquennial period of the celebration and the season of the year in which it fell. The Ancient Olympic Games were connected with divinities, which must have been personifications of astronomical powers, not agricultural ones. Victors in the games posed as embodiments of the sun and moon.

As we said before, without the twelve volumes of *The Golden Bough*, the magic behind the ancient games would remain a secret of the gods alone. However, I must admit I disagree with Frazer's statement that the Olympics were not connected with the fertility rituals. In my reading, all avenues directed me to the conclusion that the Ancient Olympic Games were indeed a thanksgiving to ensure fertility. In fact, I'm convinced that the most important games of ancient Europe were all based on a common ritual. The Capitoline Games, Lughnasadh, and the Ancient Olympics—all tried to please the same gods, according to the same schedule, and they all involved basically the same sporting events. One old saying is that "Two never happens without three." And each of these ritual games also embodied a mythology celebrating the tripartite cycle of life: birth–life–death.

The beginning of the Ancient Olympics

From hunting to farming—the origins of the Olympics.

The agricultural revolution reawakened religious fervour. The innovation of cereal cultivation had a cumulative effect that induced changes in the economy and social order and also stimulated the development of sporting and religious festivals, including the Ancient Olympics.

With the advent of agriculture, man developed more complex technology and forms of social organisation than before, and became better equipped to respond not only to the challenges of the environment, but also to his spiritual needs. As people had more time to spend on themselves, religion flourished, and with it the associated sporting, religious, and cultural festivals.

The beginning of cereal cultivation in the lowland areas of the Near East during the 7th and 8th millennia BC produced for the first time communities that were large and permanent enough to develop brick and stone architecture for private and public buildings, alongside which a whole range of crafts also sprang into being. The first civilisations arose in the fertile alluvial basins of the major rivers that water the otherwise arid plains of southern Asia, which drain from the mountain fringes where agriculture first began. Urban life and civilisation emerged in Mesopotamia (around 3500 BC) and Egypt, and soon spread to Elam, in modern-day Iran, and to the Indus Valley, Crete, and parts of Asia Minor, which constitutes the bulk of modern-day Turkey.

The development of writing

The invention of writing, also around 3000 BC, was of fundamental importance to the development of civilisation, and hence to our ancient games. It gave humans the ability to pass messages over long distances, making it possible to organise large populations through central government. It also provided the means to record knowledge and pass it down through the generations.

The spread of writing came from two main sources: Mesopotamian cuneiform and Egyptian hieroglyphics. These two systems introduced the idea of writing to Crete, which eventually developed its own linear scripts. An alphabetic cuneiform, Ugaritic, became an ancestor of the alphabet taken over by the Greeks and passed on to the Romans to form the basis of modern European script. Most of what we know about ancient history, and hence the Olympics, is due to the ancient authors who wrote in the scripts of these two great languages—Latin and Ancient Greek.

The beginning of the Olympics

Despite the tradition that 776 BC marked the first Ancient Olympics, it now seems reasonably certain that the festivals were instituted before that time. Now, we know that they were repeatedly interrupted, and several times renewed, the first time by Iphitus, prince of Elis (884 BC). In one version of this story, Iphitus asked the oracle for a way to end the war between his own city and the cities of Sparta and Pisa. He was advised to go and look for the sacred olive tree, which would be adorned with delicate cobwebs, and to restore the games and use the sacred branches to make garlands with which to crown the victors. Iphitus went back to Olympia and found the olive tree, built a wooden fence around it, and organised a meeting with the Sparta and Pisa, where the three cities would decide to select their best athletes to compete for the prize of an olive garland.

Aristotle, born in the first year of the 99th ancient Olympiad (384 BC) at Stagira in Macedonia, made mention of this remarkable tree, the cutting of whose branches were preceded by a religious ceremony. Priests would form a circle around this tree and cut the branches into a white cloth, making sure that the foliage never touched the ground. The garlands supposedly increased the strength and endurance of the victors that received them, and since the tree was a gift from the gods, it was expected that if the foliage touched the ground it would lose its cosmic power. To receive the Olympic olive crown was the ambition of every athlete, whether in the 7th century BC or the third century AD.

Here, obviously, we are confronted with an Indo-European ritual—we know that the Druids performed the exact same ceremony when they cut branches of mistletoe from an oak tree.

The Olympics were at first a fertility ritual

The harvest and the sowing of the seed were the main ritual festivals of the ancients, whose gods were the protectors and givers of fertility. The octennial, quinquennial, and triennial cycles, and the insertion (intercalation) of twelve additional days and nights into the calendar were extraordinary rituals of thanksgiving that reinforced the annual return of fertility.

The octennial cycle was an attempt to reconcile solar and lunar time. Frazer knew that the conjunction of the sun and moon was regarded as the best time for marriages and for fertility, while the quinquennial and triennial cycles gave rise to the Saturnalia and kindred festivals, which were early attempts of Aryan peoples to correct the lunar year by intercalating an extra month at intervals of several years, instead of intercalating twelve days each year.[1]

In India, the Aryans of the Vedic age appear to have adopted a year of 360 days, divided into twelve months of thirty days each, and to have remedied the annual deficiency of five days by intercalating a whole month of thirty days every fifth year.

---

[1]James Frazer, *The Golden Bough*, vol. 4 (Cambridge: Cambridge University Press, 2012), 342.

The Greeks also knew how to adjust the calendar, and adopted a similar quinquennial period for the Olympiad—the pentaeteris. The Celts of Gaul, as we also learn from Frazer, also adopted a five-year cycle but managed it differently: they intercalated a month of thirty days every two-and-a-half years so that in each cycle of five years there was a total of sixty intercalary days—equivalent to twelve days annually.

The Hera Games

Every pentaeteris at Olympia, the girls had a festival of their own in honour of Hera, the goddess of marriage. Some writers say that the festival of marriage had its origins in the time of the wedding of Hippodameia and Pelops.

The Hera games only had one type of event: the foot race, with competitors divided into three groups—children, adolescents, and young women. The first two groups raced only thirty-two metres, while the women raced 160 metres. The winners were crowned with olive garlands and given the right to eat a portion of the young cow sacrificed to Hera. Here, again, we see a ritual held in common with the Celts—the right of the champions to the first portion. The famous Celtic fights over the champion's portion are a ritual that goes back to the roots of the great Indo-European cultural family.

According to the polytheistic Greek religion, Gaea, the earth, was born of Chaos and gave birth to Ouranos. Gaea and Ouranos then conceived the Titans, of whom Cronus, patron of the harvest, became the father of the first generation of Greek gods, including Zeus. The ancient Olympic ritual preceded the time of reaping and gathering corn and other grain, and the Hera games at Olympia are another clue that the ancient Olympic festival was indeed related to fertility. In mythology, after Zeus dethroned his father, Cronus, Heracles organised the games in honour of *his* father, Zeus.

The god whose name in Ancient Greek was spelled Khrónos was associated with *time*. The word *métron* meant *measure*, so today, joining these words, in the modern Olympics we use a "chronometer"—an instrument that measures time accurately, in spite of motion or variations in temperature or humidity. In the ancient Olympics, by contrast, timing devices were never used, as time was irrelevant to the outcome: if you did not come first, you lost. Rather than the precise, minuscule divisions that are important to us today, for the Greeks time meant the passing of the seasons, with whom Cronus was also associated through his association with the harvest.

Heracles–Hercules–Alcides

Al A root connected to altitude—height.

Cides (The god's) seeds.

Seed The impregnated and matured ovule of a plant; fecundating fluid of male animals, semen.

Heliolatry

Our ancestors reverently worshipped the splendour of the sun. Though they did not have today's scientific knowledge, they understood very well that the sun played an indispensable role in raising crops. The myth of the universal deluge recalls the sky, absent the sun, shuddering with terror and loathing, and because they lived in constant fear that the sun might cease to appear, our ancestors established rituals aimed at making it shine, timed according to observations of its movement.

This kind of thinking gave rise to the most important games of ancient Europe, including but not limited to the Ancient Olympics. In examining the Ancient Olympic Games, we can see how these sporting rituals developed gradually in conjunction with changes in religion. In fact, our attempt to answer the seven sacred Olympic questions will lead us to understand the consequences of these religious developments.

The ancients considered the annual return of fertility to the earth, in which it triumphed over barrenness, as one of the major features of life. Because they believed the gods were guardians of the cosmic power, to ensure good crops they organised festivals of thanksgiving, according to what they believed the gods' needs were. The Capitoline and Ancient Olympic Games, and Lughnasadh, were all bound together by a common Indo-European culture and shared traditions of thanksgiving for the first fruits of the harvest.

7. *Olympia and the Bible*

Long before Christianity, male deities had already supplanted the goddesses worshipped in an earlier era. Palaeolithic goddess-worship was overcome by the neolithic patriarchal dominator gods.

In the beginning, religion was the cult of motherland, vegetation, and sun. At Olympia, the priestess of Demeter was the only woman permitted to attend the games, and even though the new ruler of Olympus, Zeus, was male, the table from the Temple of Hera was used to present prizes to the victors. When confronted with much older rituals, pagans always adjusted ancient traditions to the new, and showed great insight in doing so.

The great Greek goddess Demeter is equivalent to Connacht or Conna, the motherland of Celtic mythology. Demeter gave mankind the first seeds of wheat, and taught us to till the soil and make bread from the grain. In mythology, she disguised herself as an old woman and became nurse to Demophon—the son of Celeus, king of Eleusis—whom she tried to make immortal. This gives us a parallel to Celtic mythology, where the legendary Lugaidh Laidhe, eventually high king of Ireland marked himself as a future king by sleeping with a hag, who then became a young woman who was beautiful like the sun. Demeter and her daughter Persephone are personifications of the annual return of fertility.

The second phase of the Olympic holy ritual is connected to the biblical deluge, the myth of which recalls the sky without sun, shuddering with terror. The seven sacramental occurrences take place after the deluge as a ritual of thanksgiving for the new accord between gods and mankind, and for the recreation of vegetation upon the earth. When the dove brought back a freshly plucked olive leaf, the scions of humanity—whether led by Utnapishtim of the Babylonians, Manu of the Indians, or Noah of the Hebrews—knew that regeneration had begun.

Holidays, festivals, and games

Humans have a deep-seated propensity to observe natural cycles with festive solemnities, suspending the ordinary business of their lives on certain days to cherish the recollection of an important event or to unite external circumstances with their internal feelings. Indeed, this solemnisation of festivals is evidence of the nobler nature of man. Animals, guided only by instinct, pursue the same course from day to day, while man introduces variety into his life by exalting some days above others. So it is that we find him observing festivals peculiar to specific families, places, nations, and religions.

Festivals

All religions institute festivals that cherish and renew religious life, and no religion has preserved perfect independence from those that went before it. Older religions inexorably exert influence on new ones, even by opposing them. The traces of early primeval religions are undeniable in pagan ones, through which they influenced even Christianity. In trying to win over pagans, Christian teachers sometimes tried to overcome prejudices by consenting to an unholy mixture of Christian and pagan festivals. So we should not be surprised to find that the festivals Christians observe today often have pagan counterparts.

The Ancient Olympic Games

To fully comprehend the meaning of ancient sporting rituals, we must understand how religion and its theories develop over time. This happens in three distinct phases:

1. People worship the powers of all agencies and forces in creation—the motherland, the sun god, the trees, the rivers, and so on—frequently by visualising them in non-human shape. They commemorate the annual return of fertility as the major event of life, and the belief in constant death and regeneration creates rituals associated with dying gods and kings. The old saying, "Two never happens without three," is associated with the tripartite cycle of life—birth, life, death.

2. Anthropomorphism is introduced (*anthropos*: Greek, "human being"; *morphos*: Greek, "shape"), and a pantheon of deities arises in human form, with supernatural powers and human weaknesses. These gods are born, fall in love, become jealous, get married, have children, and

die. Some, like Apollo, are beautiful; others, like the Titans, are ugly.

3. Monotheistic religion arises, with its concepts of confession and the forgiveness of sins. A variety of deities is replaced by a single ruler whom no one can see, but must be followed faithfully.

In the story of the Ancient Olympic Games, first we see the unfolding of the second phase, and then, finally, in their destruction we see the movement to the third phase. The modern Olympics are under the guidance of a different phase entirely, following the dollar and a new pantheon of gods in the form of the International Olympic Committee.

8. The history of Greece

Tradition has it that the Pelasgi, led by Inachus, were the first people to wander into Greece. They dwelt in caves, supporting themselves on wild fruits and eating the flesh of their enemies, until Phoroneus, king of Argos, introduced civilisation to them. Pelasgus in Arcadia, and Aegialeus in Achaea, worked at the same time to civilise their savage subjects. The Cyclopean walls were their work.

Small kingdoms arose: Sparta and Athens. Some barbarous tribes received their names from the three brothers, Achaeus, Pelasgus, and Pythius, who had led colonies from Arcadia to Thessaly, and from Graecus (son of Pelasgus) and others. Deucalion's flood (1514 BC), and the emigration of a new people from Asia, the Hellenes, produced great changes. The Hellenes spread themselves over Greece and drove out the Pelasgi, or mingled with them, and theirs became the general name for Greeks.

Greece now raised itself from its savage state and improved still more rapidly after the arrival of colonists from Phoenicia and Egypt. About sixty years later after the Deucalian flood, Cadmus the Phoenician settled in Thebes and introduced knowledge of the alphabet. Ceres, from Sicily, and Tritolemus, from Eleusis, taught the country agriculture, and according to mythology Bacchus planted grapevines. The Egyptian fugitive Danaus came to Agros, and Cecrops to Attica.

45

Now began the heroic age, to which Heracles, Jason, Pirithons, and Theseus belong, along with the old bards and sages, including Thamyris, Amphion, Orpheus, Linus, Musaeus, Chiron. A warlike spirit filled the country, so that every quarrel called all the heroes of Greece to arms. This is the age of the wars against Thebes (378–362 BC) and earlier against Troy (c.1200 BC). This latter event is one of the principal milestones in the history of Greece; it deprived many kingdoms of their princes and produced general confusion, which the Heraclidae used to their advantage to possess themselves of the Peloponnesus, eighty years after the destruction of Troy.

The Heraclidae drove out the Ionians and Achaeans, who took refuge in Attica. But when they did not find sufficient room there, in 1044 BC Neleus led a colony of Ionians to Asia Minor, where Aeolians from the Peloponnesus had already settled, followed eighty years later by a colony of Dorians. In other states, republics were founded: in Phocis, in Thebes, in Asiatic colonies, and at length in Athens and many other places, so that for the next four hundred years, the whole south of Greece was divided mainly into republics.[1]

The prosperity of the Asiatic colonies, and the fineness of their climates, made them mothers of arts and learning. They gave birth to the songs of Homer and Hesiod. There, commerce, navigation, and law flourished. Greece retained its ancient simplicity of manners and was still unacquainted with luxury. If the population of any state became too numerous, colonists were sent out. In the seventh and eighth centuries BC, the powerful colonies of Rhegium, Syracuse, Sybaris, Cro-

---

[1]"Appleton's New Practical Cyclopedia," http://www.archive.org/strea m/appletonsnewpraoohagagoog/appletonsnewpraoohagagoo (accessed May 01, 2016).

tona, Taretum, Gela, Locris, and Messena were established in the southern part of Italy.

The small, independent states of Greece needed a common bond to unite them, and they found it in the temple of Delphi, the Amphictyonic Council, and the solemn Panhellenic golden circuit, of which the Ancient Olympic Games were the most distinguished and which also included the Pythian, Menean, and Isthmian Games. The institution, or rather revival, of the Olympic Games in 776 BC marked the beginning of an era in which people would refer to the year as being part of a certain Olympiad, counting according to how many Olympics there had been since their resurgence.

The introduction of this dating system had long-lasting significance:

> Christian chroniclers continued to use this Greek system of dating as a way of synchronising biblical events with Greek and Roman history. In the 3rd century AD, Sextus Julius Africanus compiled a list of Olympic victors up to 217 BC, and this list has been preserved in the Chronicle of Eusebius. ... Jerome, in his Latin translation of the Chronicle of Eusebius, dates the birth of Jesus Christ to year 3 of Olympiad 194, the 42nd year of the reign of the emperor Augustus, which equates to the year 2 BC.[2]

The Olympiad was a period of time calculated from one celebration of the Ancient Olympic Games to another. The ancient Greeks of this period computed time from 776 BC,

---

[2] Wikipedia contributors, *Wikipedia, The Free Encyclopedia*, accessed 10 June 2016, https://en.wikipedia.org/wiki/Olympiad.

the traditional date of the first Olympics. This mode of reckoning ended when the games were abolished in 394 BC, the second year of the 293rd Olympiad. In those days, the interval between Olympic games was a *pentaeteris*, which is forty-eight moons and two intercalary months. The symbol of the modern Olympics is a design of five rings, which was found carved in a stone in the ruins of the stadium at Delphi where the Pythian Games were held. These five rings represent the quinquennial timing of the games.

The Golden Circuit

In ancient Greece, there were many local sporting events, but four major athletic and religious festivals attracted participants and spectators from throughout the Greek world. Fans of the modern Olympic Games might not be aware that they were part of the "Golden Circuit," which the Greeks called *periodos*.

A period, of course, is a division of time, or of events occurring in it. Astronomers call the time a heavenly body takes to return to the same point in its orbit a period. The *periodos* consisted of four prestigious games, each one held as part of a religious festival in honour of a deity. The Ancient Olympic Games, at Olympia, were held in honour of Zeus, and the Pythian Games at Delphi were in honour of Apollo. Both took place once a pentaeteris. The Nemean Games in Argos, also held in honour of Zeus, and the Isthmian Games at Corinth, which honoured Poseidon, were held according to a triennial cycle.

By the fifth century BC, the Golden Circuit was firmly established.

The Pythian Games

The Pythian Games were one of the great Grecian games, instituted in early times in honour of Apollo, conqueror of the mythical serpent, Python. Celebrated initially in the Crissean field near Delphi (formerly called Pytho), they were at first held every eight years but later, by the command of the Amphictyonic Council, they were held every pentaeteris. Poems in honour of Apollo were sung to the music of the flute or lyre, and poets contended for the prize, which in the beginning was a crown of oak but later was replaced by wreaths of laurel.

The laurel

Laurus nobilis is the classical laurel, sacred to Apollo, and in the form of garlands, it is the classic symbol of victory and honour. Today, the most well-preserved forest of laurels (*Prunus lusitanica*—the Portuguese laurel) is situated on the Portuguese island of Madeira and known as the Laurissilva Forest.

It is said by some that the gods themselves contended in the first Pythian solemnity, where Castor obtained victory at horse racing, Pollux at boxing, Calais at running, Zetes at fighting in armour, Peleus at throwing the discus, Telamon at wrestling, and Heracles in the *pankration*[3]—and that all of them were honoured by Apollo with crowns of laurel. But others say that at first there was nothing but a musical contest where he who

---

[3] A no-holds-barred fighting contest similar to mixed martial arts.

sang best the praises of Apollo took the prize, at first of silver or gold but later changed to a garland.

In the third year of the 48th Olympiad, flutes were introduced: before then they had not been used at the Pythian Games ceremony. The first to win this prize was Sacadas of Argos; the councillors of the Amphictyonic League were the judges in the contests. Other musical and gymnastic contests were added afterward.

In later times, these games were celebrated in other Grecian cities, and were kept up at Delphi as late as the third century AD. The Romans are said to have introduced their own version of the Pythian Games and called them *Apollinares Ludi* in honour of the god Apollo. In later times, these games were celebrated in other Grecian cities, and were kept up at Delphi as late as the third century AD.

In fact, I also strongly believe that the Romans introduced the Pythian Games or *Apollinares Ludi* into my father's city, Lisbon: when one arrives there by international train, the last station is Santa Apolónia, a reference to the time when the pagan gods became Christian saints.

The Nemean Games

The Nemean Games take their name from a famous site in Argolis, near the present-day town of Nemea, and originated as funeral games in honour of Opheltes, the son of King Lycurgus and Queen Eurydice, who was killed in his youth by a dragon. The seven heroes who went to Thebes called Opheltes *Archemorus* (the beginning of sorrow). The festivals of Opheltes had the peculiarity of taking place every three years, rather than five.

Another account relates that the Nemean Games were established by Heracles in honour of Zeus after he had destroyed the Nemean lion. A third story combines the two origins, saying that the games originated in the funeral games of Archemorus, but were renewed by Heracles in honour of Zeus.

Today, the plain of Nemea is uninhabited—not even by a single shepherd. The Doric columns of the Temple of Zeus stand in the centre, with ruins scattered around.

The Nemean Games were less solemn than the Ancient Olympics or the Pythian Games, though sometimes, not very often, you can hear of time being divided by Nemeads, in the same way as it was divided into Olympiads and Pythiads. These games were partly gymnastic (corporeal) and partly musical (intellectual), and resembled the Olympics in their regulations. The judges of the combats, (*agonothetae*), were chosen from Argos, Sicyon, and Corinth, and wore black mourning garments in commemoration of the celebration's funereal origins. They were known for their impartiality. The *Chronicle* of Eusebius gives the second year of the fifty-third Olympiad as the first of the Nemeads. According to the poet Pindar, originally, the rewards of the victors were wreaths of olive branches, but afterwards they were of green ivy.

Agony

Our word *agony* derives from the Greek *agonia*, meaning anguish or struggle, and from *agon*, a contest or struggle.

Agony Extreme bodily pain.

Anguish Mental pain, or the effect of extreme distress.

The Isthmian Games

The Isthmian Games took their name from the Isthmus of Corinth, the narrow strip of land that connects the Peloponnesus to the Greek mainland, which was consecrated to Poseidon and where the games were held.

On one side of the Temple of Poseidon where they were celebrated, there stood the statues of the victors, and on the other a grove of pines. In the temple stood four horses, gilded all over but for their ivory hooves. Beside the horses were two Tritons, the upper parts of which were gilt while the rest was ivory. Behind the horses was a chariot, in which were statues of Poseidon and Amphitrite in gold and ivory. Not far from the temple, there were a considerable theatre and a stadium of white stone.

According to common opinion, the Isthmian Games were founded in honour of Melicertes (also known as Palaemon), whose mother Ino had thrown him into the sea, along with herself, when pursued by her murderous husband Athamas, king of Boeotia. Others say that Theseus established the games in honour of Poseidon—that they had originally been held at night, and perhaps fallen into disuse, when Theseus restored them and ordered that they should be celebrated during the day.

As Theseus, hero of Athens, was either the founder or restorer of the games, the Athenians had precedence in them. All of Greece took part except the Eleans, who had been threatened with a curse if they should ever participate. The story went that as the sons of Actor were riding to the Isthmian Games, they were killed near Elis by Heracles. Their mother, Melinōe, who then lived in the territory of Argos, discovered the murder and demanded an explanation from the Argives, who did not want to get involved. She then went to the Corinthians and asked them not to allow the Eleans to compete in the Isthmian Games as they had destroyed the peace during a sacred time. No one reacted, so she said she would curse the Eleans if they ever participated in the Isthmian Games.

The Isthmian Games were celebrated twice in each Olympiad, with the same splendour as the Olympian and other public games. The athletic exercises were the same, and the victors were at first adorned with wreaths of pine branches, then later with wreaths of dried and faded ivy, and then the pine wreaths were finally restored once again.

Olympia: City of religion, art, and sport

Although the ancient Greeks borrowed key elements of their aesthetic traditions from Egypt, they were still perhaps one of the most imaginative peoples in history. Their poetic feeling is expressed in all their works, and everything they looked at and loved was endowed with spirit and life.

A divine spirit seemed to have entered Olympia, which, according to Pausanias, was peopled with gods. The woods, streams, and fountains were filled with immortal and lovely things, and the heavens above and the earth beneath were infused with the spirituality in which the Greeks believed. Pliny says that in his time, there were as many as three thousand statues of the gods and victors in the games collected at Olympia, along with temples, altars, tombs, and treasure-houses full of votive offerings—all the most precious works of Grecian art. The great temples of Zeus and Hera, along with many smaller temples and sacred objects, were situated there around a quadrangle surrounded with walls, about 1,800 feet long and 1,500 wide. This district was known as the Altis, a corruption of the Elean word meaning "grove", and outside it there were a hippodrome for racing horses and chariots, a stadium for foot races, a theatre, and a gymnasium.

Pausanias

Pausanias was a Greek geographer who lived in the second century AD, during the reigns of Hadrian, Antoninus Pius, and Marcus Aurelius. He was a native of Cesares in Cappadocia and studied under the celebrated Herodes Atticus, a Greek aristocrat who served as a Roman consul. Pausanias taught in Athens and afterwards in Rome, where he died. In the journal of his travels, he describes everything that was remarkable about the Greece of his day, including temples, theatres, and tombs. It is an invaluable work: though he has been accused of giving information that came second-hand from anonymous manuscripts, he is nevertheless one of the great sources for us to consult on the ancient games. His work has been translated into many languages.[4]

---

[4]See for example Pausanias, *Descriptions of Greece* (trans.W. H. S. Jones), and R. E. Wycherly, *A Guide to Greece* (1955), which is a companion volume

A receptacle for miracles

The Greek temples were raised for the worship of the gods, but later, they became places to worship the miracles of art. Gods were wrought in marble, ivory, and gold. Pilgrims and worshippers approached less to behold the majestic beauty of Athena or the stern sublimity of Zeus than to wonder at the structure that contained them. Life and thought were impressed on sculpture and painting.

---

containing illustrations and an index.

9. Olympia, city of art

Sculpture–Architecture–Religion.

Architecture is the elder sister of sculpture, and the first object of sculpture was the ornamentation of temples. The word *statue* is derived from the Latin *statuo* (to set up) or from *sto* (to stand). Before Daedalus, statues were extremely primitive—the bottom half of the body of a statue was merely a cylindrical pillar and the head and torso were placed on top of it.

With Daedalus, in Greek mythology an Athenian architect and great inventor, a new epoch in art begins, about three generations before the Trojan war. Of him, the Greeks said hyperbolically that his divine genius made statues walk, see, and speak. The Greeks considered him not just the master of art, but rather its inventor.

Daedalus was also a symbol of mining, through the fable of the Daedelian labyrinth at Crete and the horizontal passages cut in the first mine there. His disciples were called his sons, and so all artists were symbolically named *Daedalides*.

The arts flourished in the temples, not only by means of statues, but still more by *anathemata* (consecrated presents that could be given as dedicatory gifts to the gods), consecrated presents, thrones decorated with figures, shields, tripods, and vases. The coffer of Cypselus in Olympia was highly celebrated. Athens produced more splendid works in twenty years than Rome produced in seven centuries.

The influence of the great poets of the time, and of religious fervour, can be seen in the art of the period, and was certainly important for Olympian architecture. This was the age of classic models and the ideal style. Phidias made two chief idols—one of Athena for the Parthenon at Athens, and the famous statue of Zeus at Olympia. Both were wrought in ivory and gold.

The Zeus at Olympia, one of the Seven Wonders of the Ancient World, was beautifully formed, and forty feet high. One epigrammatist wrote that "The statue of Jupiter [Zeus] would have thrust off the roof of the Temple like a thin shell, if it had ever risen from its golden throne." The god sat upon a splendidly adorned throne, and his expression united power, wisdom, and benevolence. He sat as the chief judge of the contests in the Olympic Games.

Phidias began the school of ideal forms: male figures sculpted were afterwards often gods, demigods, and heroes. Myron was another celebrated sculptor, who flourished about 443 BC. He was particularly happy imitating nature, and made a cow so much lifelike that even bulls were deceived and approached her as if she were alive. He modelled his classic sculptures on the ideal of Heracles and formed the ideals of the whole animal kingdom, only one hundred years after Phidias. The word *Myron* has itself survived to have a greater influence: in the Portuguese language *mirone* means onlooker or bystander, and one can say of a person, "*ele tem uns grandes mirones*" ("he is a great observer"). Myron's athletes were also much celebrated, particularly his *Discobolus* (*Discus thrower*), who supports his left hand on his knee and, bending, prepares to throw the discus with his right hand raised backwards.

The sculpture of Greece, which was at its height of glory in arts and in arms during the days of Phidias, surpasses the art of all other nations. The whole land was filled with trophies of war and with statues of heroes and gods. Wherever one turned, one's eye would be charmed by the loveliest and noblest forms the mind of man could conceive, or his hand give form to. The rudest minds of Greece looked with reverence on such works, and serfs and peasants wandered among groves of statues without injuring them.

Some works of high merit by the succeeding great sculptors of Greece have descended to us without suffering much damage from accident or time, but the gold and ivory creations of Phidias were a temptation that the barbarian conquerors of Greece could not resist. The wooden figures perished in fires, and the brass or silver statues of Praxiteles and Polycletus were broken into pieces, melted, and used for coin or capacious drinking cups. Such is the fate of all works of art made of precious materials.

Procession

In the Roman Catholic Church, a procession is a solemn march of the clergy and people, around the altars and churches or in the streets, to return thanks for a divine blessing or to avert a calamity. As part of the symbolic worship of nature, processions had been in use among the ancient heathens, too, who formed solemn processions about fields that had been sown, sprinkling them with holy water to increase their fertility and protect them from injuries.

The festivals in honour of Zeus (Jupiter), Lugh, and other

divinities, among the Greeks, Romans, and Celts, were solemnised with processions in which the images of the gods were borne about. Such processions appear to have been introduced into the Christian Church in the time of St Ambrose, Bishop of Milan, in the fourth century. In Protestant countries, processions, as well as pilgrimages, have ceased.

The Olympics, naturally, were commemorated with a procession, which began three days before the commencement of the games and ran along the sacred way to Olympia from the city of Elis, a distance of roughly sixty kilometres. At its head walked the judges (*hellanodikai*) and other officials, followed by the athletes and their trainers, their families, and then free-born citizens, barbarians, and last of all, slaves. Each had their own place in the procession and gave their own offerings.

The heralds

In ancient Greece, each city state had its own calendar, so to announce the starting date of any festival, they sent out heralds in advance to spread the news. The origins of heralds are as ancient as those of priests. There was nothing like our modern-day technology for communication, so heralds were found in all societies.

The Romans had three types of heralds: the *caduceatores*, who were the same as the Grecian heralds and were heralds of peace; the *fetiales*, who were heralds of war and peace; and the *praecones*, who were criers of the superior magistrates.

The caduceator carried certain plants, such as verbena, myrtle, olive branches, and rosemary, in his hand as a symbol of his office, and for his security. Among the Grecians, he carried a wand of laurel or olive—the *caduceus*. The Athenian herald carried a wand bound with wool and ornamented with various fruits. The Greek appellation of this kind of herald was derived from Ceryx, son of Hermes and of Pandrosus, daughter of Cecropos, from whom the Athenian heralds originated. The Spartan heralds must have been derived from Talthybius, the herald of Agamemnon, who was worshipped in a temple in Sparta.

The *fetiales* formed a college of twenty members, established by Numa Pompilius, the second king of Rome, after Romulus. These heralds also had a diplomatic character: their department was everything connected with the declaration of war and the making of treaties. If war was decided upon, they solemnly proclaimed it. If Rome considered herself injured, the *fetiales* demanded satisfaction, and if the request was not complied with in a period of thirty days, they would go again to the hostile frontiers, throw a bloody spear, and declare war, according to the demands of a solemn formula called the *clarigatio*. The *fetiales* wore sacred verbena as a wreath around their heads, and if they were sent to conclude a treaty, they carried a flint.

The *praecones* were employed to proclaim matters of public interest to the people at religious ceremonies, in the *Comitia*, at public sales, judicial trials, in the Senate, on the publication of laws (which they read out), and at funeral games. In Portugal, during the festival of St Anthony, we construct wooden stages decorated with palm leaves, for musical bands, and we still call these leaves *verbenas*.

10. The games: Five days of courage and strength in an effort to achieve victory

The events of the Ancient Olympic Games

- Chariot racing
- Horse racing
- Foot races of
    - one *stadion* (approximately 200m)
    - two stadia (400m)
    - four stadia (800m)
    - twenty-four stadia (4,800m)
- Discus
- Broad jump
- Javelin
- Pentathlon
- Wrestling
- Boxing
- Pankration

Victoria: goddess of victory

Victoria was the Roman equivalent of the Greek goddess Nike. Daughter of the Titan Pallas and the goddess Styx, and the sister of Zelus (Zeal), Bia (Force), and Kratos (Strength). She is generally represented with wings, a laurel on her head, and a palm branch in her hand.

Horse and chariot racing

The hippodrome

The word *hippodrome* derives from *hippo* (horse) and *dromos* (course or race). Among the Greeks, Romans, and Celts, hippodromes were public places where horse and chariot places were held. Of all the hippodromes of Greece, the most remarkable was the one at Olympia, of which we have descriptions from Pausanias, though there is some confusion about its characteristics. For instance, *Wikipedia* states:

> According to Pausanias, it was situated to the south of the Stadium and covered a large area about 600 meters long and 200 meters wide. The hippodrome was a wide, flat, open space where the starting point and the finish line were designated with a pole and a second smaller pole called *nyssa* designated the turning point.[1]

---

[1] Wikipedia contributors, "Hippodrome of Olympia," *Wikipedia, The Free Encyclopedia*, accessed https://en.wikipedia.org/wiki/Hippodrome_of_Oly

However, archaeologist Olympia Vikatou gives this account of the hippodrome's measurements via Pausanias:

> Pausanias, who visited Olympia in the second century BC, describes the monument (VI, 20, 10–21) as a large, elongated, flat space, approximately seven hundred and eighty metres long and three hundred and twenty metres wide (four stadia long and one stade four plethra wide, according to Pausanias). The elongated racecourse was divided longitudinally into two tracks by a stone or wooden barrier, the embolon. All the horses or chariots ran on one track towards the east, then turned around the embolon and headed back west. Distances varied according to the event. The racecourse was surrounded by natural (to the north) and artificial (to the south and east) banks for the spectators; a special place was reserved for the judges on the west side of the north bank.[2]

In the future we will eventually have the correct dimensions as archaeologists are today using sophisticated geomagnetic technology to study the hippodrome.[3]

The great hippodromes of the ancients

The Circus Maximus of Rome was the most remarkable racing venue of the ancient world, but the Hippodrome of Constantinople approaches it in splendour. This latter structure

---

mpia.

[2] Olympia Vikatou, "Hippodrome of Olympia," *Odysseys*, accessed 30 June 2016, http://odysseus.culture.gr/h/2/eh251.jsp?obj_id=552.

[3] DPA News Agency, "German Archeologists Locate Olympian Hippodrome," *Deutsche Welle*, 27 July 2008, http://www.dw.com/en/german-archeologists-locate-ancient-olympian-hippodrome/a-3499778.

still fills travellers with astonishment. Septimus Severus began the Hippodrome's construction, and it was completed by Constantine the Great, in imitation of the circus of Rome. It was surrounded by two ranges of columns, extending further than the eye can see, resting on a broad foundation and raised one above the other.

The Hippodrome was adorned with immense quantities of marble, porphyry, and bronze, forming statues of men and beasts, emperors, and athletes. Among other remarkable monuments, the four bronze horses of Lysippos once stood there, which had migrated from Greece to Rome, then to Constantinople. Afterwards, they were taken to Venice and Paris, and at last back to Venice.

The Turks call the Hippodrome the *Atmeidan*—the sacred horse-place—recalling its ancient purpose. At present, it is 400 geometrical paces in length and 100 in breadth. It is almost quadrangular, and passes over many slight irregularities. The corroding effects of time notwithstanding, some remarkable relics of antiquity are still found there.

Chariot racing: An extremely hazardous sport

The chariot race was the opening event of the Ancient Olympics, and was held in the hippodrome at Olympia, which was a large, flat, open space, and roughly rectangular—not the curved track of today's harness races. According to Pausanias, the track was 600m long and 200m wide; the starting line and two turning posts at either end marked the course. The chariots were released from a special starting gate called the *aphesis*.

Chariot races were of differing lengths, of one to twelve laps, according to class. The two-horse chariot for colts and the mule-cart race were only three laps each. The four-horse chariots raced the full twelve laps, and apparently up to forty chariots could take part in each race. The chariots themselves were strongly, even elegantly built, but were not well adapted to speed. Since swinging four galloping horses 180 degrees around the turning posts sent the chariots skidding wildly, many collisions occurred, making charioteering an extremely hazardous sport. In a typical race, very few charioteers managed to finish the twelve laps.

At Olympia, charioteers wore a long white tunic; they were the only clothed athletes competing in the games. The victor's crown was not presented to the successful charioteer, but rather to the owner of the chariot and horses. Charioteers were considered only drivers; they were employed in much the same way as racehorse owners now employ jockeys today. At one of the most famous horse races in the world, the Melbourne Cup, the prizes are still given to the owners of the horse, not to the jockey. And apparently, the Australian jockeys' costume is inherited from the glorious chariot races of the Celts.

Unlike the other sports at Olympia, then, chariot racing was primarily for people with money. A rich man could have various charioteers racing for his team, and in fact, only chariot racing had a team competition. A chariot owner could manage to have his chariots finish first, second, *and* third, taking multiple honours.

The Roman racecourse

The typical Roman racecourse, or *circus*, was an oblong building in which public chariot races took place, alongside exhibitions of pugilism and wrestling. One short side formed a half circle, at the opposite end to the entrance. Spectators sat on both sides and at the curved end, with the seats rising gradually like steps, resting on strong arches. At the foot of the seats, there was a broad ditch, called the *euripus*, whose purpose was to prevent wild beasts from leaping among the spectators.

At the centre of the racecourse was an arena covered with sand, where the games were held. It was divided lengthwise into two parts by a wall (*spina*) twelve feet thick and six feet high, which was adorned with little temples, altars, statues, obelisks, pyramids, and conical towers. Of the towers, which were called *meta*, there were three at each end, which served as goals, and around which the circuits were made. By the first *meta*, opposite the curved end of the circus, there were seven other pillars with oval balls at their summits. One of these balls was taken down for every circuit that the racers made of the track.

On the outside, the circus was surrounded by colonnades, galleries, shops, and public places. The largest such building in Rome, the Circus Maximus, was in the eleventh district of the city, which was itself sometimes called Circus Maximus, and was on the spot where Romulus held the games at which the Sabine women were carried off. The *ludi magni*, a kind of ritual games, were also celebrated there.

Tarquinius Priscus designed this great building, and some of the wealthy senators completed it. The historian Dionysius of Halicarnassus gives its length as 9,331⅓ feet, and the breadth as 2,187 feet. According to Pliny, it could hold 200,000 spectators, while Aurelius Victor said it could hold 385,000. Julius Caesar enlarged and ornamented it, and then under Nero it was burned down and under Antoninus Pius it was pulled down. Trajan rebuilt it and Constantine made further additions to it.

Nowadays, few vestiges remain of the Circus Maximus, and the circus of Caracalla, in the first district, is in the best state of preservation.

In Rome, charioteers were mostly slaves, who by competing had the chance to become rich and famous—or to die young. In ancient Rome, a slave who became a champion driver could not only buy his freedom but could even become a national hero. The greatest such champion was Gaius Appuleius Diocles, a Celtiberian who went from slave to multimillionaire, and whose name and remarkable achievements were even carved on a monument in Rome. A legend of the track, he raced for more than twenty-four years, winning 1,462 four-horse chariot races in his career.

Athletics

Foot races

In the Ancient Olympics, the Greeks never included the marathon. The longest distance the athletes ran was the *dolichos*—the long race, twenty-four times the length of the Olympic stadium. We get our word *stadium* from the Greek *stadion* (also sometimes romanised as *stade*), a length of 600 feet. At Olympia, the stadium is 192.28 metres long, but at Delphi it is 177.36 metres—because the distance varied according to the length of the individual foot used to make the measurement.

There were multiple kinds of foot races at Olympia. The one-stadion race was equivalent to the modern 200 metres, and the winner of this race was called the *stadionike*. To become a *stadionike* was a great honour, since the race was surrounded with mystical connotations. In fact, the event gave the name to the *stadion* as a unit of distance, and also to the greatest sporting arenas of modern times. In English-speaking countries, the word also gives a name to men of noted sexual prowess: "stud". The two-stadion race was known as the *diaulos*, and was equivalent to the modern 400 metres.

The *hippios*, or four-stadion race, matches today's 800 metres, but though it was part of the roster of events on the Golden Circuit, some authors say it was never included at Olympia. At Olympia there were only the *triestes*: the *stadion*, the *diaulos*, and the *dolichos*. This last event, of twenty-four stadia, is nearly equivalent to the modern 5,000m. An armed *diaulos* was also introduced in 520 BC, at the sixty-fifth Olympiad. The marathon was introduced only at the modern Olympic Games, commemorating the messenger Pheidippides' famous—and fatal—run from Marathon to Athens to announce the Persians' defeat at the Battle of Marathon.

Discus

Among the Greeks and Romans, the discus was a disc of stone or metal, convex on both sides. Throwing it was one of the gymnastic exercises, and in the Olympics and at other games it was considered a great honour to win this contest. Perseus is said to have invented the discus, and in mythology, the hero Hyacinth was killed while trying to catch a discus thrown by his lover Apollo. The discus also has a cosmic significance: in astronomical terms, *disc* is used to mean the face of the sun and moon as they appear to observers on the earth.

The broad jump

The broad jump, which was the historical name for today's long jump event, was a type of jumping contest included in the roster of events on the Golden Circuit. In the Ancient Olympics, at least, the Greeks never did the vault jump, perhaps because it was not practical on a battlefield, where the leap often occurred in war. Today, around the world, the armed forces still use this type of jump, and Portuguese and Australian troops include it as a part of their training.

Javelin

The javelin, also known as a lance or spear, must be the most primitive weapon men have developed for hunting and fighting. Though a separate event in the modern games, in the Ancient Olympics it was only included as part of the pentathlon. This was a sport particularly well adapted to warfare, which is no doubt the main reason it was included in the games.

Five martial events: The pentathlon

According to myth, the hero Jason, leader of the Argonauts, organised five events in honour of his friend Peleus, winner of first place in the wrestling and of second place in all the rest of the games the Argonauts organised on the isle of Lemnos.

The pentathlon (from *penta*, the Greek for five) was designed to test the skill of athletes in a wide range of areas. According to recent research, it is likely that at first only three events were part of a predecessor to the pentathlon: the broad jump and the discus and javelin throws. To these, running and wrestling—which were also present as standalone contests at Olympia—were added to make up the full pentathlon. The foot race in the pentathlon was one stadion of 192.27m. Wrestling took place around the altar of Zeus, and was, apparently, mainly used as a last resort to determine the final victor if one had not clearly emerged from the other four events.

The pentathlon was first introduced at the eighteenth Olympiad in 708 BC, and the first winner was Lampes of Lacedaemon (later Sparta). In fact, the Lacedaemonians were the favourites in the pentathlon, thanks to the renowned rigour of their training. From the beginning of the Olympics, Spartan soldiers won many victories in the games.

Once athletes became professional, though, generalist soldiers no longer won victories over these specialist competitors. We can compare this with the situation of the present day: a soldier from the Australian SAS, which is among the best of the world's special forces, could hardly stand up to Stan Longinidis, an Australian kickboxing champion of Greek descent. They would be likely to beat him in the first four events, but would be likely to then be beaten in the final (and determining) wrestling event. And over thousands of years, the basic physical and mental training of a soldier hasn't changed very much, though the weaponry they use has.

To be a winner in the sacred games was the dream of every Greek athlete, but to be a pentathlete, or the victor of the pentathlon, was a task for demigods. Because of their beautiful and well-trained physiques, winning pentathletes were often a model for sculptors.

War games

The games, which had started as a fertility ritual, evolved into games of war. The Greeks believed that sport was valuable martial training as well as a way of honouring the gods, and looking at the events of the pentathlon, we can see how well the skills they tested could be adapted to warfare.

Other events with a martial character included the *hoplitodromos*, a partially armoured foot race, was a serious test of soldiers' endurance. Instituted in the 65th Olympiad in 520 BC, this race had competitors running naked, but wearing a helmet and greaves and carrying a shield, for a distance of two stadia. Ancient authors tell us that twenty-five shields were kept in the temple of Zeus, perhaps to ensure the fairness of the competition by making them all carry the same weight.

The modern Pentathlon

The modern pentathlon was included in the Stockholm Olympics of 1912, and was adapted to the warfare of the time— just before the first world war. The event simulates the process of a soldier delivering a message: he starts on horseback, dismounts, and enters a duel with swords. Avoiding danger, he has to fight his way out, shooting with a pistol. Then he jumps into a river, swims across to the banks, and runs through the countryside.

Boxing

Greek mythology attributed the sport of boxing to divine origins.

Boxing, or pugilism From the Latin *pugil.*

Pugnacious Quick to argue or fight.

Pugilist A boxer.

Pugnar To fight or struggle.

Pujanca (Portuguese) Vigorous, powerful.

Punho (Portuguese) Fist.

Pugnus (Latin) To fight with the fist.

> As the reader may understand, the word *boxing* must be derived from the time when pugilism was confined to the boxing ring. Because of the technical difficulties involved in building a round ring, at the beginning of the century, the organisers decided to make a square ring or box.

Ring Anything in the form of a circular line or hoop.

> The closest approximation to an actual, circular boxing *ring* that I've ever seen is the octagonal ring made by the Kung Fu Association of Australia.

Pugilism has been a well-organised sport for thousands of

years. In Mycenaean Greece and Minoan Crete, boxing competitions were part of the religious ceremonies. But in the Olympic Games, boxing became one of the main attractions.

The sport was introduced at the 23rd Olympiad n 688 BC, and the first victor was Onamastus of Smyrna, who also formulated the rules of the sport. The boys' event was introduced at the Olympiad of 616 BC. In the ancient games, the sport had no weight divisions, so most boxers were of big stature. But there were still two categories: juniors and seniors. In the modern Olympics, there are no age divisions: juniors compete along with seniors in every sport. In Greece, males more than twelve but less than eighteen fell into the junior division, which is equivalent to our modern junior divisions for boys aged fourteen to eighteen.

Though the Greeks had Chronos, the god of time, boxing matches had no time limit: they could go on until one competitor was knocked out or raised his forefinger in capitulation. Some successful boxers—famous Olympic champions such as Dorieas, Eucles, Theagenes, and Polydamas—acquired an almost mythical status, and became very rich.

The famous boxer Diagoras of Rhodes not only became wealthy, but also achieved something like demigod status. A famous athlete of exceptional stature, he won six times at the Olympic Games, twice at Nemea, and four times at the Isthmian Games. Between them, his three sons won five victories at Olympia, and his two grandsons were successful at Olympia and Delphi. Writing in the second century AD, Pausanias recorded that statues of Diagoras and his sons and grandsons were to be seen displayed at Olympia, and modern archaeology has discovered their bases. Pindar's First Ode to the Olympics, written in 476 BC, was widely esteemed. It was said to have been displayed in letters of gold in the temple of Athena at Lindos in Rhodes.

Dorieus, the eldest son of Diagoras, had himself won three victories at Olympia. In the year 406 BC, fifty-eight years after the victories of Diagoras, when the Athenians were engaged in the final and bitter stages of their long, disastrous war with Sparta, Dorieus was captured by the Athenians in a sea battle. Although at that time it was customary to release prisoners of war for a ransom or put them to death, the Athenians asked for no ransom for Dorieas—they set him free immediately.

Rich and famous

Two and a half thousand years ago, great boxes were also millionaires, just like today. Olympic champions, just as today, could make substantial sums outside of the Olympics. In the ancient period, this money came mainly from competing in private games.

We can get some idea of the size of the prize money in these private competitions by looking at the wages of a Greek soldier or skilled labourer—around one drachma per day. By comparison, a boxing champion could win two and a half thousand drachma—almost seven years' wages—in a single bout. In fact, we can compare Diagoras to the present Mike Tyson, who in 1996 made $75 million and was the world's highest-paid sportsman, leaving Michael Jordan in second position and Michael Schumacher in third. The top forty highest-paid athletes that year included other boxers: Evander Holyfield (6th, $15.5m), Roy Jones Jr (12th, $12m), Riddick Bowe (15th, $11.5m), Oscar de la Hoya (175h, $11.3m), Julio Caesar Chavez (25th, $9m), and

George Foreman (36th, $8m). In some respects, society hasn't changed much in the last 2.5 millennia.

Wrestling

According to the Olympic records, the sport of wrestling first appeared in the 18th Olympiad, in the year 708 BC, which also included the pentathlon. Boys' wrestling arrived only in the 41st Olympiad, in 616 BC. According to Greek mythology, the sport had many sources: some attribute it to Theseus, who fought with Cercyon, and others to Heracles. In one myth, Heracles originated wrestling when he fought the Nemean Lion with his bare hands. But others claim that Hermes invented the sport, while according to Philostratus, it was Palaestra, daughter of Hermes.

The contact sports were not played in the gymnasium, but in the *palaestra*, the Greek word for the wrestling school. This was a courtyard surrounded by columns, connected to the gymnasium. At the Olympic contests, wrestling took place not in the stadium, as other sports did, but around the altar of Zeus.

Many authors tell us that the sport was a symbol of the contest of right against wrong. Others said that the victor in the wrestling challenge had to combine grace, style, and skill. But we hear neither from the ancients nor from contemporary authors why the Olympic wrestling challenges took place around the altar of Zeus. Only by listening to the voice of the pagan gods can we hear a conclusive explanation.

Pankration

Pankration was the highlight of the Golden Circuit. Introduced in the 33rd Olympiad in 648 BC, the contest was first won by Ligdamus of Syracuse. Pindar, one of the most energetic and sublime poets of ancient Greece, sang the victors' praises, and his poems are among the most beautiful of what remains in ancient literature. Forty-five are dedicated to the Golden Circuit: fourteen in celebration of the Olympic victors, twelve in honour of the Pythian victors, eleven to the Nemeans, and eight to the Isthmians.

We know that the Celts also incorporated *pankration* into their Lughnasadh games because the Celtic victor of the context was called the *Catorix*—from *cato* (*pankratio*) and *rix* or *ri* (king)—making them the "king of combat."

Pindar

Pindar was born in Boeotia, in or near Thebes, in the 65th Olympiad, about 520 BC. In time, he became so renowned that Alexander the Great spared the house he lived in when the city was destroyed. The Spartans had done the same when, earlier, they entered Thebes in triumph. Even in Pindar's lifetime, his fellow citizens are said to have erected a statue in his honour.

Eight of Pindar's odes are dedicated to *pankration*: from them we have the names of the famous pancratists. Reading Pindar, we also learn that in his time, as in ours, the sport was not suitable for anyone past their physical prime.

Winners of the pankration in Pindar's odes

Nemea II Timodemus of Arhanae.

Nemea III Aristocleides of Aegina.

Nemea V Pytheas of Aegina—winner of the youths' pankration. 489–88 BC for both the victory and the ode.

Isthmia IV Melissus of Thebes.

Isthmia V Phyladidas of Aegina.

Isthmia VI Phylakidas of Aegina. The date of this victory cannot be fixed with any certainty.

Isthmia VII Strepsiades of Thebes.

Cleandrus was also a winner at the Nemean Games. Other famous pancratists included Lygdamus of Syracuse; Doreis, son of the famous Diagoras of Rhodes; Theagenes of Thasos; Polydamas of Scotussa; Protophanes of Magnesia; and Cleitomachus, a boxer and pankration victor.

Keeping records in the ancient games

How did the Greeks manage to keep sporting records without the sophisticated instruments available to the modern Olympics? Though we might ask this question, it was not that important to the ancients how far the athletes threw the spear or discus, or how fast they ran the races. The most important thing was to win—to beat one's opponents in the contest. In the original Olympics, there were no awards for second or third place. If you didn't come first, you lost: there was no second-best.

The other coveted achievement was to secure the title of *paradonikes* (winner of two or more events on the same day) or *periodonikes* (winner in all four games of the Golden Circuit: Olympic, Pythian, Isthmian, and Nemean). Some successful athletes gained an almost mythical reputation. Theagenes of Thassos won six events in four Olympics between 478 BC and 456 BC, including three in his last: wrestling, boxing, and pankration. Sostratos of Sikyon six times at Nemea, six at Isthmia, twice at the Pythian Games and three times at Olympia. Kleitomachos of Thebes won three times in the Isthmian Games in wrestling, boxing, and pankration.

Alexander the Great and the demigods of Alexandria

Greeks, Macedonians, and Celtic warriors under the leadership of Alexander the Great took the art of *pankration* from Europe to India. From our modern point of view, we can see history repeating itself: finally the Europeans would get *pankration* back from abroad, when they had long forgotten it.

During the reign of Alexander, the games became more international. Athletes came from as far as Egypt to compete at Olympia. To win the wrestling and the pankration in the same

Olympiad was a feat supposedly only for gods or demigods—the likes of Heracles. But in fact, some athletes—Aristomenes, Marion, and Aristones, for instance, all of Alexandria—did achieve this feat.

As the conqueror of a vast empire, Alexander was a great leader and military strategist, and known as a courageous soldier who always led his own soldiers into battle. He was born in Pella, Macedonia, in 356 BC. His mother was Olympias, the daughter of Neoptolemus of Epirus, and his father was the king of Macedonia, Philip II, from whom Alexander learned his martial skills.

At this time, Macedonia was inhabited by the Tracicines—who whom the Paeonians and Pelagonians belonged—and the Dorians, to whom the Macedonians were believed to have belonged to on account of their language and customs. The Macedonians were civilised long before the rest of the Greeks, but the Greeks later surpassed them and eventually came to see them as semi-barbarous.

Macedonians were allowed to compete in the Olympics only because the Macedonian royal house was descended from Heracles. The Heraclide clan was the most prestigious in the Greek world.

The famous phalanx, so successfully used by Greeks and Macedonians in Alexander's campaigns, had been introduced by Alexander's father at the Battle of Chaeronea in 338 BC. As part of this new unit of warfare, armed with four-metre-long pikes (the *sarissa*), foot soldiers could hold off the enemy and leave the cavalry free to charge. With these tactics, Philip II defeated Athens and Thebes, and having been elected chief commander of the Greeks, was preparing for a war against Persia when he was assassinated in 336 BC.

Alexander, not yet twenty, ascended the throne and punished his father's murderers before going into the Peloponnesus and receiving, in the general assembly of the Greeks, the post of commander in the war against Persia. This was to be the start of his empire.

He crossed into Asia in 334 BC with thirty thousand foot soldiers and five thousand horsemen. At the crossing of the Granicus River, he defeated the Persian army commanded by Miltridates, the son-in-law of Darius III, king of the Persians. The second of Alexander's great battles with the Persians took place near Issus, and this victory opened the whole of Persia to him. Darius was an inexperienced leader compared with Alexander, who had fought under his father many times. Alexander broke the immense Persian army with a charge of the phalanx, and the Persians fled in wild confusion.

Tyre, the famous Phoenician city, resisted Alexander but was taken after seven months and was destroyed. Alexander continued his victorious march through Palestine, where he surrounded all the towns except Gaza, which like Tyre was destroyed. Weary of the Persians, Egypt received Alexander with open arms, and to confirm his power in the region, he founded Alexandria, which became one of the most important cities in antiquity and today is Egypt's second largest.

Gaugamela

Despite the immense numerical superiority of his enemy, Alexander routed the Persians immediately at the Battle of Gaugamela. He aimed to take Darius prisoner, but the king was on a chariot in the midst of his bodyguards and fled, leaving his army, baggage, and immense treasures to the victors. Later, Darius was murdered by Bactrian nobles, bringing the Achaemenid dynasty to an end.

After Gaugamela, Babylon and Susa, the richest cities of the East, opened their gates to Alexander, who then directed his march towards Persepolis, the Persian capital. Alexander hoped to gain the affection of the Persians by adopting their dress and manners, but was disappointed. In Persia, Macedonian and Greek troops were discontented; Alexander married Roxanne, daughter of the Bactrian nobleman Oxyartes, and encouraged his soldiers to marry Persian women to unite their people with the Greeks and Macedonians.

Intoxicated by success, Alexander marched victoriously to India, where he established Greek colonies and built several towns—among them Bucephala, named after a horse of Alexander's that had been killed in battle. He meant to advance to the Ganges, but his army's discontented murmurings compelled him to return. While planning a campaign to Arabia, he suddenly became ill after a banquet and died a few days later in Babylon, in 323 BC.

Alexander's reign was a critical period in human history. His career was not one of empty conquests; he spread the language and civilisation of Greece in his wake. He opened the road from Europe to India, and products from the East flowed westward. Under his generals, known as the Successors, Greek kingdoms persisted in Asia for centuries.

A warrior and a gentleman

Not only a warrior, Alexander was also a brilliant diplomat. When Alexander was born, his father, Philip II, thanked the gods for allowing his son to be born in the time of Aristotle, disciple of Plato. From the age of thirteen, the boy had the great philosopher as his tutor, and was instructed in all branches of human knowledge, especially those necessary for rulers. Aristotle's books on ethics, politics, and rhetoric, in particular, treat of the subjects that would have been most important to Alexander. Aristotle sought to cultivate in his pupil the talents and virtues of a military commander, and it is said that even during campaigns, Alexander never lay down without having read a few pages of his tutor's writing.

Marathon

In 490 BC, Athens was on the verge of being destroyed by a foreign army. "Come and help fight the *barbaros*,"[4] was the message that Pheidippides most likely gave the Spartans after running all day, a distance of 125 kilometres. His effort was wasted: on his return journey he ran back to Athens with the message that the Spartans were willing to send forces but the Athenians must delay the battle for five days.

Though the Spartans were not afraid of war and wanted to help, they also scrupulously respected a religious belief that prevented them from acting before the full moon. They arrived

---

[4]Barbarians—for the Greeks *barbaro* was the word for one whose language was unintelligible.

the day after the battle, by which time the Greeks had been victorious, thanks to the tactics of the general Miltiades.

The Battle of Marathon

Some of the Greek generals, disheartened by the Persians' superior numbers, had wished to wait for the Spartans to commence battle, but Miltiades favoured an immediate attack. Aristides and Themistocles supported him, along with some of the other generals. The chief general, Callimachus, was still concerned about the plan, but Miltiades prevailed.

Each of the ten tribes of Athens had placed a thousand soldiers under the direction of a commander, and this small army of ten thousand advanced to the plains of Marathon, where another thousand soldiers of their allies, the Plataeans, joined them. Miltiades then drew up his troops at the foot of a mountain in a wooded plain, to impede the advance of the Persian cavalry.

The Plataeans occupied the left wing, Callimachus commanded the right, and Aristides and Themistocles the centre. Miltiades himself was everywhere he was needed. In spite of the Persians' immense numerical superiority, he began the attack at full strength, and though the Persians defended themselves with cool obstinacy, after several hours both wings gave way. In the centre, the Persian general Datis pressed Aristides and Themistocles hard with his best troops, but the Greeks attacked him in the rear. The Persians were then in a general rout: those who escaped the sword fled to the waves, where many of them nevertheless fell into Greek hands.

The Persians lost 6,400 men, the Athenians just 192. Miltiades himself was wounded but survived. In recent times, archaeological excavations at Olympia unearthed an ancient, conical helmet dedicated to the Medes, an Iranian people, which may have been the helmet Miltiades wore at Marathon, and an offering of thanks to the Olympic gods for his victory over the Persians.

Sparta

Sparta is known as the ancient city of warriors and of the sacred shield. Spartan mothers always farewelled their sons before they departed to war with the words, "Here is your shield. Come back either with it or upon it."

Sparta, or Lacedaemon, was the capital of Laconia (aka Lacedaemonia) and of the Spartan state. It lay on the west bank of the river Eurotas, and embraced a circuit of forty-eight stadia, or about six miles. The ruins can still be seen, and are now called Palaeopolis: the ancient city. The city was irregularly built, and consisted of five separate quarters that were still not enclosed by a common wall by the 120th Olympiad.

Among other remarkable places in Sparta that Pausanias describes, the marketplace was one of the most distinguished, and contained the public buildings where the magistrates held their meetings. The principal ornament of this marketplace was the Persice, a colonnade built of spoils taken from the Persians, whose roof was supported by statues of the Persians. There was also the *chorus*, where the *ephebi* danced; the *gymnopaedia*, adorned with statues of Apollo, Diana, and Latona; the Baroneta, where resided the kings of the family of Eurysthenes; the Leschai, two halls where popular assemblies were held, the Lesche of the Crotnes near the tombs of the Agides and the Lesche

Paecile; and finally, the temple of Minerva Poliouchos (Chalcioecus) on the Acropolis.

The Spartans were distinguished among the peoples of Greece by their manners, customs, and constitution. Their kings ruled only by popular will, and had no other political privileges than of giving their opinion first in the assemblies, acting as umpires in disputes, and commanding the army. Their material advantages were a large share of the spoils of war, and then chief seats at assemblies and meals.

The Spartan people, descendants of the Dorians, who gained possession of Laconia under the Heraclidae (descendants of Heracles), were preoccupied mainly with war and hunting, and left agricultural labour to the Helots, but the Lacedaemonians, or Perioeci (the ancient inhabitants of the country) also engaged in commerce, navigation, and manufacturing. Although the Spartan conquerors were more refined and cultivated than the Lacedaemonians, the arts of industry flourished only among the latter, who gradually mingled with the less numerous Spartans and became one people with them.

Herodotus estimated the number of Spartans at only eight thousand, and with the Lacedaemonians they formed a single state, with a national assembly, to which the towns sent deputies. Military contributions, in money and troops, formed the main tribute that the free Lacedaemonians paid to the Dorian Spartans. But the Lacedaemonians' jealousy of the Spartans occasionally divided the two groups, and during the Theban war several Lacedaemonian towns withdrew their troops from the Spartan army and joined Epaminondas.

The Spartans' distinguishing traits were severity, resolution, and perseverance. Defeat never discouraged them. But they could be faithless and crafty. We can see this from their conduct in the Messenian Wars, where they not only bribed the Arcadian king, Aristocrates, to betray the Messenians, but also corrupted the Delphic oracle, having the predictions of its priestesses altered to make use of them against their enemies.

Lycurgus set the age at which Spartans could contract marriage as thirty for men and twenty for women. When a Spartan woman was pregnant, pictures of the most handsome young men were hung in her room to produce a favourable effect on her womb. According to Homer, it was an early custom for Spartan women to employ wet nurses to preserve the beauty of their breasts. These nurses were treated as part of the family.

A newborn Spartan child was brought forth upon a shield, it is said, and, if male, was laid without swaddling clothes to leave him free use of his limbs, on that shield with the words, "Either with this or upon this." While other Greeks washed their newborns with water and afterwards rubbed them with oil, the Spartans bathed them in wine to try the strength of their constitution. They had the notion that a wine bath produced convulsions or even death in weak children, but confirmed the health of the strong.

If an infant proved vigorous and sound, the state received it into the citizenry. If not, it was thrown into a cave on Mount Taygetus. In the other Grecian states, exposing children to the elements was a matter of custom, but in Sparta the law forbade it. Yet, Spartan children were early introduced to hardships and became accustomed to freedom from a young age. To accustom the children to hunger, they gave them little food, and if they needed more they were obliged to steal it—but they were severely punished if caught, not for the theft but for their lack of skill in its execution. Every ten days they were required to present themselves before the *euphoria* (inspection), and whoever was found to be too fat received a flogging.

Wine was not generally given to girls in Greece, but was commonly allowed to boys from their earliest childhood, with Sparta no exception. There, the boys were obliged to wear their hair short until they attained the age of manhood, when it was allowed to grow. They usually ran naked and were dirty, as they did not bathe and anoint themselves like other Greeks. They took pride in having the body covered with bruises and wounds, and wore no garments, except in bad weather, and no shoes at any time. They were obliged to make their beds of rushes from the Eurotas.

Until their seventh year, male children were kept in the *gymnasium*, in the care of the women; from seven to eighteen they were called boys and to the age of thirty, youths. In their thirtieth year the Spartans entered the period of manhood and enjoyed the full rights of citizens for the first time. But before that, from seven, the boy was withdrawn from parental care and educated under the public eye, in the company of others of the same age. If any person withheld their son from state care, they forfeited their civil rights.

The renowned Spartan martial education

Physical education was the principle object of attention for Spartan boys and youths, and consisted of gymnastic exercises, running, leaping, discus-throwing, wrestling, boxing, the chase, and *pankration*. These were performed naked in buildings called *gymnasia*. Besides gymnastics, the young Spartans also practiced dancing and military exercises.

One of the more curious Spartan customs was the flogging

of boys (*diamastigosis*) on the annual festival of Diana Orthia, to inure them to pain. A priestess stood by with a small and very light wooden image of Diana, and if she observed that a boy was scared, she called out that the image of the goddess had become so heavy she could not support it, and the blows were redoubled. The men who were present exhorted their sons to fortitude, while the boys tried to surpass each other in stoicism. Anyone who cried during the scourging, which was so severe it was sometimes fatal, was considered disgraced, while those who bore it without shrinking were crowned and received the praises of the whole city. According to some it was Lycurgus who established this ritual of Diana. Others attribute it to the period of the Battle of Plataea in 479 BC.

As mentioned, Spartan children were encouraged to practice theft in certain cases, but if detected they were flogged, obliged to go without food, or compelled to dance around an altar singing songs of self-ridicule. The fear of shame in being discovered sometimes led to extraordinary acts. One boy who stole a young fox concealed it under his clothes to avoid detection, and endured it scraping and gnawing through his bowels—which of course proved fatal—rather than allow the theft to be discovered by letting the fox escape.

Among the Spartans, swimming was considered so essential that there was a proverb to the effect that a man who could not swim was good for nothing. Modesty of deportment and concision in speech were also thought essential virtues. The term *laconic* is named for Laconia, the Greek region that included Sparta, and signifies a curt, pithy manner of speaking that was a signature of the Spartans.

The Spartans were the only people of Greece who avowedly despised writing, and they excluded it from the education of their youth. Instead, the whole of their instruction consisted of learning obedience to their superiors, endurance to all hardships, and a resolve to conquer or else to die in war. And yet, however ferocious their reputation, the Spartans were carefully instructed in knowledge of their laws, which were taught orally without being reduced to writing.

Peculiar democracy

Democracy is a Greek word: *demokratia* comes from *demos* (people) and *kratos* (strength or power). But the democracy practiced by the ancients differs completely from that of today.

Democracy may be seen as a worn word, nothing more than a fallacy. But in fact the Greek words *demos* and *agogos* (leading), when put together, gave the demagogues avenues to spread pure demagoguery. As in the past, we see today's leaders making use of prejudices and false claims and promises to gain power.

In our view, democracy's major feature is to manipulate the emotions of the masses using a strategy of demagogical domination. Therefore, we should never confuse democracy with human rights. The word doesn't represent the system as it should. It can be described as a paradox.

According to August Boeckh, in *Die Staatshaushaltung der Athener* (Berlin, 1817), Athens and the islands of Salamis and Helena contained a territory of 847 square miles, with 500,000 inhabitants—365,000 of which were slaves. He estimates there were 180,000 residents of the city and harbour of Athens itself, and the mines nearby had 20,000.

The statesmen Cimon and Pericles (444 BC) made Athens

elegant, but Pericles also laid the foundation for a future corruption of manners. Both Plato and Plutarch were critics:

> Plato rejects the glorification of Pericles and quote as saying: "as I know, Pericles made the Athenians slothful, garrulous and avaricious, by starting the system of public fees". Plutarch mentions other criticism of Pericles' leadership: "many others say that the people were first led on by him into allotments of public lands, festival-grants, and distributions of fees for public services, thereby falling into bad habits, and becoming luxurious and wanton under the influence of his public measures, instead of frugal and self-sufficing".[5]

Athens' statesmen and generals also protected the soil against foreign invaders, and the Athenians boasted of being an ancient and unmingled race. They called themselves sons of the soil they dwelt on, and pretended that they had originated with the sun.

The earliest inhabitants of Athens were savages, living in scattered huts without even bread or marriage, until the time of Cecrops, who came with a colony from Sais at the mouth of the Nile. He is considered Athens' first real king: he softened their manners and taught them a better way of living. He planted olives, and showed the Athenians how to cultivate grains. He also instituted worship of the gods, commanded the people to offer sacrifices of their produce, established laws for marriage, and directed the burial of the dead.[6]

---

[5] Wikipedia contributors, "Pericles," *Wikipedia, The Free Encyclopedia*, accessed 30 June 2016, https://en.wikipedia.org/wiki/Pericles.

[6] The source for much of this section is Francis Lieber and E. Wigglesworth (eds), *Encyclopædia Americana* (New York: G & C. & H. Carvill, 1829), starting from p.455.

At that time, the inhabitants of Athens numbered about 20,000, and as their king, Cecrops divided them into four classes, compelled them to gather their dwellings together, and protected them from the attacks of robbers by having a wall erected around the settlement. This was the story of the origin of Athens, which was then called Cecropia.

One of Cecrops' descendants founded eleven other cities, and in later times he made them unite and make Athens the capital of the whole confederacy. He also founded the great feast called the *Panathenaea*, which was a religious, sporting, and cultural event similar to the Olympics but organised by the city of Athens in honour of their goddess Athena:

> The Panathenaic Festival (Panathenaia) was Athens's most important religious celebration and the second oldest one in the region. During the festival inhabitants of Attica (Panathenaic means "all-Athenian") and other parts of the empire honored the goddess Athena Polias's birthday (who had leaped from the head of Zeus, according to myth). Since Athena was the city's protector, the whole festivity had great religious and political significance.[7]

As head of state, this descendant of Cecrops watched over administration of the laws, and commanded the army. At this time, the people were divided into the classes of noblemen, husbandmen, and mechanics. Magistrates were selected from among the nobles; they performed the duties of priests, and interpreted the laws. This descendant embellished and enlarged Athens, and invited foreigners to help populate the country.

---

[7]"Panathenaic Festival," *Ancient World History*, accessed 30 June 2016, http://earlyworldhistory.blogspot.com.au/2012/02/panathenaic-festival.html.

After the death of Codrus in 1068 BC, the Athenian monarchy was abolished. It had continued for 487 years from the time of Cecrops. An archon, chosen for life, from then on possessed the king's power. After a further 316 years, the archons' term of office was limited to ten years, and then seventy years later it was limited again to just one year, and their number increased so that there were nine archons instead of one.

At this point, the Athenians still lacked a regular code of laws. The archon Draco was commissioned to draw one up, but its severity—from which we take our word *draconian*—dismayed the people. In 594 BC, Solon introduced a milder legal code along with a better constitution, which provided that the government should continue to be democratically elected, and that it should be administered by a senate of four hundred members, chosen from among the people.

Solon divided the people of Athens into four classes once again, this time according to their wealth. The offices of government were to be filled from the first three of these ranks. Under Solon, too, the Peloponnesian War began, which ended with the conquest of Athens by the Lacedaemonians.

As the vanquished, the Athenians were subjected to mortifying conditions. The Lacedaemonians placed thirty supreme magistrates over the city, whose rule, upheld by the occupying garrison, was arbitrary and cruel. After eight dreadful months, Thrasybulus overthrew the magistrates' tyranny and restored both freedom and an improved version of the old constitution. Then Athens began to elevate herself among the states of Greece once more, and was fortunate to make an alliance with Thebes against Sparta.

But this new period of Athenian power did not last long. A more dangerous enemy even than Sparta arose in the north.

The Athenians had opposed Philip II of Macedon in the Phocian war, and because of that he took possession of some of the Athenian colonies. Though the Greeks took up arms against Philip, they were defeated at the Battle of Chaeronea, effectively making Philip the leader of Greece.

After the death of Philip's son, Alexander the Great, the Athenians attempted to regain their freedom; on failing, they were obliged to receive a Macedonian garrison in the harbour of Munychia. Antipater, then leader of the Macedonians, ordered that only citizens with an estate of more than 2,000 drachma should take part in the administration of the government. Soon after, Athens was taken by Antipater's son Cassander, who restored the oligarchy and named Demetrius of Phaleron governor. Demetrius quietly enjoyed this office for ten years, but the Athenians, who hated him because they had not chosen him, called Demetrius Poliorcetes, who eventually became king of Macedon, to their aid.

This latter Demetrius took Athens, restored its ancient constitution, and received extravagant honours from the citizens. But when Alexander the Great's *Diadochi* (Successors) went to war against him and he went out to meet them at the Battle of Ipsus in 301 BC, the Athenians refused to let him back into the city. Again he conquered Athens, in 294 BC, forgave the citizens for their resistance, and permitted them liberty, only placing a garrison in Munychia and the Piraeus.

Eventually, the Athenians drove out these garrisons of Demetrius, and Athens for a long time maintained its freedom until it was conquered again by Antigonus Gonatus. Athens then remained subjected until it separated itself from the Macedonians and joined the second Achaean League. The league united with the Romans against Philip V of Macedon, and Athens' new allies confirmed its freedom.

Yet, when the Athenians allowed themselves to be misled into supporting Mithridates against the Romans, they drew vengeance upon themselves. Sulla captured the city and left it only a semblance of liberty, which it retained until the time of Vespasian, under whom Athens became a Roman province. Once the Roman Empire became divided, Athens belonged to the East. In 396 AD it was captured by Alaric the Goth, and the country was devastated.

Christianity and the decay of Olympia

The splendour for which Olympia was once known has now completely vanished. When Christianity rose, heathen Olympus fell—though not at once, still slowly and surely.

The first Roman emperor to convert to Christianity was Constantine the Great. In the year 313 AD he published the famous edict of tolerance in favour of the Christians (the Edict of Milan), and made attempts to settle the Arian controversy. In 394 AD, another Roman emperor, Theodosius the Great, who was profoundly influenced by Bishop St Ambrose of Milan, stopped the reckoning of time in Olympiads. The next year he forbade every heathen festival, including the Olympics.

Oracles became melancholic; divine voices were no longer heard in Olympus; incense no longer ascended to the gods, and new light was directed to the great and invisible God, of whose existence the heathens had but glimmerings.

Constantine the Great

Caius Flavius Valerius Aurelius Claudio Constantine, now known as Constantine the Great, was born in Naissus (now Serbia) between 274 and 280 AD. Constantine was the son of the future emperor Constantius Chlorus and his wife or concubine, Flavia Helena, whom he abandoned when he ascended to the rank of Caesar in 293 AD. When Constantius was associated with Diocletian as part of the tetrarchy that governed the empire, his son Constantine was kept as a hostage at Diocletian's court, where he was educated with the greatest care.

After Diocletian and Maximian Hercules had laid down the reins of government, Constantine fled to his father in Britain, to escape the machinations of the emperor Galerius. After Constantius's death, in 306 AD, Constantine was proclaimed Augustus by his army, in accordance with his father's wishes. Galerius was unwilling to allow Constantine the title of Augustus, recognising him as Caesar only.

But Constantine took possession of the countries that had been his father's subjects: Gaul, Spain, and Britain. He overcame the Franks in Gaul, took two of their leaders prisoner, and followed the rest of their people over the Rhine where he surprised and defeated them. Then he set his armies against Maxentius, who had joined Maximian in opposing him.

During his campaign in Italy, Constantine is said to have seen a flaming cross in the heavens, beneath the sun, and the cross bore the inscription, "*In hoc signo vinces*" ("Under this sign you shall conquer"). The following night, Christ appeared to him, and commanded he take as his standard an image of the fiery cross he had seen, which was called the *labarum*. Not long after this, he vanquished the army of his rival Maxentius beneath the walls of Rome, and drove it into the Tiber, where Maxentius drowned.

Olympic decay

After the fall of Corinthia in 146 BC, the Romans had carried away multitudes of paintings and statues, and filled Rome with the spoils. In 86 BC, the dictator Sulla, after plundering the sacred city of Olympia, transferred the Olympics to Rome to commemorate his triumph. After his death, the games went back to Greece.

Not every Roman emperor brought harm to Olympia. In fact, Augustus had ordered multiple improvements, even sending his son-in-law, Marcus Agrippa, to supervise the repairs and the new construction. Under Augustus, the Ancient Olympic Games regained their prestige, and throughout the period of Augustus's successors, the games had an imperial Roman flavour. Tiberius was the victor of the quadriga chariot race. Germanicus competed in the 199th Olympiad in 17 BC, and also won the quadriga chariot race.

According to the records, the most charismatic royal to compete in the Olympics was Nero, who had the ridiculous desires (for a Roman emperor, at least) to be esteemed a great musical performer and also to be a champion chariot racer. In his vanity, he broke the chronology of the Olympiad, introduced musical contests, and raced a chariot drawn by ten horses. Some authors write that Nero fell from his chariot but paid the judges to give him the victory on the grounds that if he hadn't have fallen, he would have won.

The final blow to the Ancient Olympics

The magnificence of Olympia has now been destroyed, partly because of Greece's political decay, partly by earthquakes, Roman legions, and northern barbarians. But more destructive than any earthquake, army, or barbarian horde was the rise of Christianity and the fanatical zeal of its early adherents.

When the terrible march of Christianity upon Olympia was begun, sculptures and paintings, temples, statues, and books were all trodden relentlessly underfoot. The Christians accused the Greeks of rude behaviour for competing in the nude, and argued that exposing naked bodies caused people to feel shame and injured their reputation. They claimed that sports were vicious, corrupting individuals' physical and moral well-being, and did not live up to the standards of Christianity.

Now, as we look back, we may think that the Christians had some reason to feel antagonistic towards sporting events as manifestations of a pagan religion. In fact, it is more likely that the Christians were under the spell of the Roman Colosseum.

The Roman Colosseum

The gigantic ruin of the Colosseum in Rome was once the greatest amphitheatre that Roman magnificence had ever erected. Built by Vespasian, it is said to have been completed in just one year, by harnessing the compulsory labour of 12,000 Jews and Christians. It could hold about 110,000 spectators, more than 90,000 of them seated. The enclosures in which wild animals were kept at the Colosseum are still standing, and remind us of the time when their builders were devoured by the beasts to gratify the Romans' savage tastes.

The early Christians' doctrines of moral duties

We learned before that the sacred Olympic Games were not an event involving slaughter. In fact, if an athlete accidentally killed an opponent in one of the combat events, he would be disqualified and the dead combatant posthumously crowned with the garland of victory.

When we observe carefully, we may realise that in spite of having a keenly developed moral philosophy, while the Christians ended the Olympic Games they did not stamp out the slaughter of the bloody spectacles in the Colosseum. Ironically, even the Pope attended the extravagances there.

What kind of conscience would allow the trading of slaves to die in exhibitions at the Colosseum? One man who was involved in spreading Christian morals, Pope Dionysius (who served from 259–268 AD), was also connected with such slave trading. How could such a man approve of such a trade, even in hope of large profits?

Perhaps Dionysius was possessed of the same kind of conscience that guided the Vatican in the sixteenth century, when it accepted the argument of Portuguese slave traders that black Africans had no soul, and that therefore buying or kidnapping men and women to sell as slaves was not a sin. The Vatican welcomed the idea, so long as the slavers paid for a papal bull.

If they could be amenable to slaughter and slavery, why would Christianity put an end to the Olympics? The answer is a matter of business interest: they did so not out of moral conviction, but because the pagan festivals were strong competition for their new church.

Olympia was not a place for people to live

Olympia was designed for worship, pilgrimages, and the sporting events of the Olympics. Today, Portugal is the only place where we can find something similar to the frenzied sporting festivals of the Ancient Olympics, the Capitoline Games, and Lughnasadh. But to construct an event of such import, we must combine events of different places together, for the spirit of the Ancient Olympics is now fractured.

For example:

- The sacrifice of the *tauro*, common to three festivals, is today the bullfight.

- The songs of Dionysus or Bacchus are now the *fado*, the Portuguese national musical tradition.

- The sacred dance of the ritual sacrifice has become the fandango, the folk dance of the river Tagus.

- *Romarias* or country fairs are still celebrated, similar to ancient times, where people get together to worship the local deity, buy and sell all sorts of things, compete in traditional games, and drink and fight. A *romaria* without a fight is not a good *romaria*.

- To see what it was like to worship the pagan gods, one can go to Fatima on the thirteenth of March. Though the goddess has become a saint, the fervour is the same.

- To taste the drink of the sacrifices, we can try Portuguese sangria.

The Bible and Olympic mythology

After diligent enquiries into the Ancient Olympics, I discovered a remarkable relationship between the seven sacramental Olympic questions and the story of the Biblical deluge. In the Old Testament, in the story where the dove returns to Noah with an olive branch (of which the Olympic garlands were made) as a sign that the floodwaters have receded, there is fuel for the view that the second phase of the Olympics was a scene portraying a ritual of fertility to please the gods in thanks for their original act of creation.

The ancient Greeks based their festivals on their sacred mythology, which was similar to the Biblical scriptures in significant ways. Once we know that Biblical writers modelled their accounts on the pagan beliefs of the Sumerians, such as those we find in the *Epic of Gilgamesh*, it is not difficult to see how the Olympic ritual was continuous with the rest of heathendom.

In fact, at the beginning of the twentieth century, the dedicated archaeologists excavating the sites of old Babylonia that were mentioned in the Bible finally received their reward when they discovered an engraved *stela*. After meticulous work to decipher it, scientists made an amazing discovery, which was that the Hebrew scribes of the Bible had taken inspiration from the thoughts, stories, and laws of a far older society, specifically, Hammurabi's Code. Hammurabi was a Babylonian king of the 18th century BC, more than twelve centuries before the books of the Old Testament were written. Beyond that, there is the possibility—which raises many questions—that the Biblical laws could have a heritage of more than 5,000 years, stretching back to the peoples who first settled what became ancient Sumer.

The Bible's Babylonian connection

The Hebrew scribes of the Bible, who lived in Babylonia, were descendants of war prisoners from the time when Nebuchadnezzar and his army brought 10,000 captives from Jerusalem. It is understandable, then, that the Biblical writers would be inspired by the grandeur of Babylonia and adapted elements of its mythology. In fact, our own civilisation is the result of the human habit of exchanging cultures.

In the ruins of Babylonia, which still engage the attention of travellers in modern times, archaeologists discovered materials traceable to the even more remote age of the Sumerian civilisation. At the beginning of the twentieth century, scientists, after careful excavation, uncovered not only the oldest literature in the world, but also written evidence that the Hebrew writers of the Bible had based their scriptures on the Sumerian law of Hammurabi:

> The stele containing the Code of Hammurabi was discovered in 1901 by the Egyptologist Gustav Jéquier, a member of the expedition headed by Jacques de Morgan. The stele was discovered in what is now Khūzestān, Iran (ancient Susa, Elam), where it had

been taken as plunder by the Elamite king Shutruk-Nahhunte in the 12th century BC.[8]

More than 5,000 years ago, the people of Mesopotamia already knew the story of the scriptures that would be sacred to the Jews and, eventually, the Christians.

Babylon/Iraq

Babylonia was an old Asiatic empire, also known as Chaldea, since the Chaldeans had control of the whole country. It is a flat region, watered by two great rivers, the Euphrates and the Tigris. The former, which is almost always level with its low banks, overflows at the slightest occasion, and inundates the country every spring when it is swollen by waters flowing from the mountains of Armenia. The Euphrates fertilised Babylonia as the Nile does Egypt.

Nature has compensated the country that was Babylon for a want of wood and stone by a plentiful supply of clay. When dried in the sun, or burned in furnaces, it makes durable bricks, and the ruins of ancient Babylonia have resisted the effects of the climate even to the present day.

According to the representations of the ancients, the extent of the old capital, Babylon, situated on the Euphrates, approached the miraculous. The walls are said to have been 350 feet high and 87 feet thick; the city had 250 towers,

---

[8]Wikipedia contributors, "Code of Hammurabi," *Wikipedia, The Free Encyclopedia*, accessed 2 April 2009, https://en.wikipedia.org/wiki/Code_of_H ammurabi, cited in "The Code of Hammurabi (Circa 1,760 BCE)," *Jeremy Norman's HistoryofInformation.com*, accessed 30 June 2016, http://www.h istoryofinformation.com/expanded.php?id=2240.

100 gates of brass, and was more than 60 miles around. The temple of Belus and the hanging gardens were among the greatest wonders not only of the city, but also of the ancient world as a whole. Today, almost every trace of them has been destroyed.

The Babylonians, one of the most ancient nations on earth, were of the Semitic race, as can be seen from their language, which is an Aramaic or Syriac dialect. They were a distinct people, with settled abodes, and a certain degree of scientific cultivation, as early as 2000 BC. In 630 BC the Chaldeans, who were a wandering people, had under Nabopolassar descended from Taurus and the Caucasus to conquer Western Asia. Led by Nebuchadnezzar, they destroyed Jerusalem in 588 BC, defeated Tyre and Phoenicia, and founded an empire that extended to the shores of the Mediterranean.

Babylonia, which even earlier had been a seat of knowledge, particularly astrological and astronomical, became the centre of an empire. Commerce and industry flourished, producing wealth and a love of luxury and magnificence. Manufacturing of linen, cotton, and silk was especially celebrated. Learning was confined to the priests.

The seven sacramental Olympic questions

1. Why were the victors in the Olympics crowned with garlands of olive leaves, when all authors on the subject explain that the games were dedicated to Zeus, the father of the gods, whose sacred tree was the oak?

2. Why did the wrestling contests take place around the al-

tar of Zeus, and not in the stadium along with the rest of the sports, and why did they have no time limit?

3. Why were the Olympiads for a long time named after the victors, runners of the stadion?

4. Why did the ancient games of Europe all originate as funeral games?

5. What did the torch relay race mean?

6. Why was a sacred truce, the *hieromenia*, strictly imposed?

7. Why were women not allowed to compete in the Olympics?

The deluge

Noah and the Bible—Rig Veda, the world's oldest scripture, describes how Manu survived the flood.

Deluge From the Latin *diluviurn*, from *diluere* (to wash away).

In Hindu lore, Manu, the first man, is said to have once found a small fish in his drinking water.

"Have mercy on my life and I will pay you back with the same pity," said the fish, and then in a prophetic manner predicted a deluge.

Manu placed the fish in a hollow vessel, but it grew so quickly he had to transfer it into a cistern, then a lake, and finally into the sea. The fish's extraordinary growth was a sign that the flood was imminent, so Manu constructed an ark, and the fish dragged this ship through the water by a rope.

After the flood subsided, Manu asked for a wife, and from his union with the woman granted him, all the generations of mankind were born.

This Indo-European fable gave rise to the Celtic story of Fintan, the salmon of knowledge. Judaism, Christianity, and Islam all subscribe to a version of the same story, with Noah in the place of Manu, and trace their heritage from the Hebrew patriarch Abraham, one of Noah's descendants.

From the time my father took obligatory lessons in Catholicism in Portuguese schools, he learned that every one of his fellow creatures was his brother. What the priest wanted to say was that we are all descended from Noah. *Irmão* is the Portuguese word for brother, but the majority of the Portuguese, without even knowing the origin of the word, call each other *manu*, which then becomes a synonym of *irmão*. Yet, to call someone *manu* doesn't necessarily mean they are literally your brother: you can call a good friend *manu*, so the term is rather one of brotherly solidarity. My father tells me he feels very proud when friends call him "*O manu Ivo*" (brother Ivo).

So, remarkably, the Portuguese have this expression referring to Manu, the survivor of the flood in the *Rig Veda*, and not to Noah, who is the hero of the same story as it appears in the Old Testament and is known to the Catholics. The lesson of this custom is that in their old-fashioned way, the Portuguese still give voice to the knowledge they have received by blood and in the pagan mythology of their ancestors the Lusitanos (Lusitanians), who were part of the great Indo-European family that lived long before the Hebrews wrote the Old Testament.

The holy man Saint Anthony was also born in Portugal, the city of my father, who believes that the story of him delivering the sermon to the fishes shows another remote influence from our Celtic ancestry.

According to the Bible, the great flood was intended to punish the iniquity of mankind. The book of Genesis says it was the result of a rain of forty days, and of the breaking open of fountains from the great deep. The flood covered the earth to a depth of fifteen cubits (6.858 metres) above the tops of the highest mountains, killing every living creature on land except for Noah, his family, and the animals, who entered the ark at God's command.

After the flood had been upon the earth for 150 days, and then subsided over an equal period, making its whole duration somewhat less than a year, Noah became convinced that land had once again emerged. A dove returned to the ark with a freshly plucked olive branch in its beak, which meant that small trees were showing above the surface of the water. Noah decided to land on Mount Ararat, in present-day Armenia.

The great flood is supposed to have occurred in the 1656th year after the world's creation, according to Petavius (2327 BC) and Mueller (3547 BC). Many other nations mention similar inundations in the mythological parts of their history, and these stories largely coincide with the scriptural account of Noah's preservation of humanity and the animals during the Biblical flood. As a result, many people have inferred that this inundation is part of universal mythology. The figures of Fohi in China, Scotivarata or Manu-Sanhita in India, Xisuthrus in Chaldea, Utnapishtim of Babylon, and Deucalion in Greece, have all been recognised as counterparts of the Biblical Noah. Even the American Indians have a tradition of a deluge followed by a renewal of the human race from the family of one person. All these people are supposed to have been saved by divine intervention and to have become the second father of mankind.

The many skeletons found petrified inside or on the tops of mountains, and the remains of animals of hot climates in countries that are now cold, have been seen as confirmations that there was indeed a global flood. With the story of Noah, the global deluge becomes not only a story of the history of all humanity, but one specifically about God's chosen people—the Israelites.

This is what the Hebrews wrote in the Bible about themselves. But long before the Bible came into being, a number of different nations had also claimed to be the mightiest or most favoured of peoples and written similar mythologies. Even the Sanskrit *Rig Veda*, the most ancient sacred scripture in the world, also gives this story. But more importantly, the *Epic of Gilgamesh*, written in cuneiform on clay tablets more than four thousand years ago, also tells the story of a global flood, and probably inspired the scribes of the Bible who lived in Babylon.

Deucalion

Deucalion was the son of Prometheus and Pandora, and the father of Helen, ancestor of the Hellenes. He led a colony from Asia into Greece, and established himself in Lycorea and on Mount Parnassus, from which he made an incursion into Thessaly and expelled the Pelasgi.

In Deucalion's time there was also a storied flood, known as the deluge of Deucalion, which occurred in the sixteenth century BC. It is described in a fable, where Zeus decided to destroy mankind by water on account of its impiety, and caused a flood by means of violent rain. Deucalion saved himself and his wife Pyrrha, and navigated the waters for nine days and nine nights. Once the flood had subsided (which they determined by sending out a dove), they disembarked on Mount Parnassus. Afterwards they consulted the Oracle of Themis to find out what they needed to do to restore mankind, and were directed to throw "the bones of their mother" behind them. Understanding that their mother was Gaea, the earth, they threw rocks behind them; Deucalion's became men, and Pyrrha's became women.

Why were the Olympic victors crowned with wreaths of olive leaves?

The answer to this, one of the seven sacramental Olympic questions, can be found in the Bible and the story of the Great Flood. When at last Noah felt the ark scrape on solid ground as it lurched and settled on Mount Ararat, Noah still did not yet dare disembark. Only the tops of the mountains had appeared above the water.

After waiting a while, he sent out a raven to see if it could find anywhere to settle. It did not return, and a week later Noah sent out a dove. It flew back on the same day, having found nowhere to rest. He waited another week, and then sent out the dove a second time. It was away all day, but when evening came it returned with a freshly plucked olive leaf in its beak. So Noah realised that small trees were showing above the surface of the water. Again he waited seven days, and then sent out the dove for a third time. This time it did not return, letting Noah know that it was time to leave the ark.

At this point, God said to Noah, "Leave the ship with your family and lead out all the creatures so they swarm on the earth and increase." God blessed Noah and his sons with almost the same blessing that he had given Adam, "Be fruitful and multiply."

Readers can see here a repetition of the original act of creation. Order or peace triumphs once more over chaos, and fertility over barrenness. Whether we consider this motif in connection with sacred history and theology, or with civil or natural history, it forms a subject of great interest. When we read the Bible and compare it with Greek mythology, or with the myths of other peoples, we see numerous connections—and also a clue to understanding why the Greeks replaced the original garland of oak leaves (sacred to Zeus) with olive branches. We also see why the olive branch and the white dove were so celebrated in the mythology of the ancients, not only by the Hebrews but also by the Celts, Greeks, and Romans, and why the dove was revered and considered a symbol of peace and humility. It is because the olive branch the dove brought back after the flood is an allegorical representation of reconciliation between gods and men.

The divine Olympic wrestling match

Why did wrestling contests take place around the altar of Zeus and not in the stadium with the other sports? Why did it have no time limit?

In the stadium, man competes against man, but in the wrestling contest, the struggle is between man and God. This contest was an allegorical ritual in which the winner represented active physical strength, holding the semen capable of impregnating the woman of destiny, the motherland.

The motherland

The Celts also had their own allegorical rituals, one of which was the wedding feast of kinship. The queen of Connacht (Portuguese: Cona) represents the motherland that conveys sovereignty. The land is poor and restless while it awaits its destined king. At this stage, the land is frequently personified by a hag who, after sleeping with the king, transforms into a young woman who is beautiful like the sun. The marvellous Munster story, handed down from early times, features the legendary Lugaidh, who distinguished himself as the future king by sleeping with the hag and transforming her.

The phrase, "beautiful like the sun" was known even to my grandfather, who never lost an opportunity to use it. When he first saw me, he said, "*A menina e linda como o sol*" ("the girl is beautiful like the sun"). I believe this is an old phrase inherited from our ancestors, because my grandfather and father were both born near a high hill overlooking the sea, called *Linda a Velha* (the beautiful old woman). The name indicates a primitive ritual, probably of pre-Celtic origin, that was familiar to the Lusitanos and observed during the Lughnasadh games. Is this destiny, or coincidence?

Today, *Linda a Velha* is situated behind the Portuguese National Stadium.

Another historical coincidence

Lugh, the Celtic sun god, is probably related to Lugalbanda, the champion of the gods of Babylon. Lugalbanda was the father of Gilgamesh, Babylon's legendary wrestling champion, whose story inspired the writers of the Bible.

An archaeological discovery of writing in cuneiform on clay tablets from around 2000 BC mentions the wrestling ritual involving Gilgamesh, a ruler from the Babylonian city of Uruk (the Biblical Erech, now Iraq) and the wild man Enkidu. The gods sent Enkidu to challenge Gilgamesh, who as a ruler was hated by some and loved by others. Their contest went on until the break of dawn, with neither man the clear victor, though Enkidu acknowledged Gilgamesh as the stronger. After their match, Gilgamesh became great friends and adventuring companions.

Here we have a story, written 1,500 years before the Bible, that sets a precedent for the Biblical story of Jacob, whose name God changed to *Israel*, which can mean "wrestles with God." Israel represents the land of the Jews, and the presence of wrestling as a common motif and ritual across these cultures proves the both Greeks and Celts knew the sacred scriptures long before the Hebrews wrote the Bible.

Wrestling in the Bible

The story of Jacob is that one night a strange adventure befell him. He had withdrawn to a solitary place, wanting to be alone, perhaps to plan what he should say to his twin brother Esau when next they met. Suddenly, in the darkness Jacob became aware of a man who challenged him to wrestle, and from the awe he felt, he knew that this was no ordinary man, and also that he had no choice but to accept the challenge. They wrestled until dawn broke, and then the mysterious being, seeing that he could not overcome Jacob by grappling, struck him and dislocated his thigh. Even so, Jacob would not let the man go until his opponent had given him a blessing. This stranger finally agreed to do so, saying, "Your name, Jacob, will be changed to Israel (striven-with-God), because you have wrestled with God and man has prevailed."

Samson

Jacob's is not the only Biblical wrestling story. According to the Bible, there came a day when the Philistines held a great festival in honour of their god Dagon. The Philistines shouted for their captive Samson to be brought to the temple so that they could mock him, but now that his hair and beard had fully grown again, all his strength had returned, and he asked the boy who led him to guide him to the pillars that supported the roof.

When he felt his arms around the pillars, he prayed, "O, God, just once, just this once, give me back my old strength." Then he strained with all his might. As he did so, the jeers and laughter of the Philistines turned first to silence, and then to moans and cries of fear. The pillars trembled, bent, and finally broke, and the roof crashed on those below, killing everyone in the temple—including Samson himself.

Milo

The Greek story of Milo also involves wrestling and a god, but in this instance the hero doesn't die—he instead saves those inside a temple. A native of Crotona in Calabria, Milo was a student of Pythagoras and one of the most celebrated Grecian athletes. He had won prizes six times in the Olympic Games, once in the boys' wrestling and five times in senior matches. He had six laurel garlands from the Pythian Games, nine from the Nemean, and ten from the Isthmian.

Milo was not only a prodigious Olympic champion, but also a famous warrior, and led the Crotonians to victory in battle against Sybarite invaders in 510 BC. Many instances are cited of his incredible strength, and in one, as a temple where Pythagoras was teaching his pupils was about to collapse, he seized the central pillar and delayed the temple's destruction until all present had escaped. Once, he carried a bull to the sacrifice on his shoulders and then killed it with a blow of his fist.

It is curious to note that Milo's strength was reportedly so great that he could kill a bull with his bare hands. Just a few decades ago, we heard that the famous Japanese karate master, Sosai Mas Ôyama, who founded the Kyokushin style, was also said to have killed a bull with a blow of his fist.

In his odes, Pindar tells us of another two famous wrestling champions: Alcimidas of Aegina, who won a boys' wrestling match in the Nemean Games around the year 470 BC. Another ode praises Theaius of Argos, who won the wrestling match at the Nemean Games along with several athletic trophies.

Remarkable international wrestling coincidences

Sumo, in Portuguese, means supreme or maximum. It also means *juice*. In the old days, wrestling matches were allegorical competitions held to purify the best juice, which held the quality of being capable of impregnating the motherland. Japan, the "land of the rising sun," is also the country of sacred Sumo wrestling.

Though superficially very different, the Japanese and the Celts shared many superstitions and rituals. The warriors of both cultures loved to cut off their enemies' heads and keep them as trophies of war. They both used two weapons—a long and short sword—and had a tradition of bravery to the point of suicide, which in Japan became known as *kamikaze*. They both also adored the swastika, a symbol of the sun, and today, the Japanese martial arts of Shorinji Kempo still use it as their emblem.

Olympic wrestling and fertility

The meaning behind the Olympic wrestling contest is directly connected with fertility. The first written record of such an event was put down, as we have seen, by the Babylonians in the *Epic of Gilgamesh*, where Enkidu and Gilgamesh are the counterparts of the Biblical Jacob and his God.

In the Gilgamesh story, the wrestling match begins at a wedding, where Enkidu challenges Gilgamesh for trying to exercise his *droit du seigneur*—the lord's right to sleep with any bride of common birth in his domain on her wedding night. There is debate about how prevalent this was in Europe: though it was supposedly a feature of medieval times, it appears there is a significant element of mythology to such stories. And yet, the custom is clearly as old as history itself, since we see it in this Sumerian episode from nearly 5,000 years ago.

The Gilgamesh and Enkidu episode appears in tablet two of the *Epic of Gilgamesh*. God sends Enkidu to challenge Gilgamesh, and like a shepherd, the wild man Enkidu guarded the door, standing ready to meet and stop the king.

Gilgamesh then came on like a wild ox, to claim the bride as his. Wild heart met wild heart, and at the door the struggle began. The two men grappled and exchanged heavy blows. They broke doors and walls, and on the street the pair wrestled wildly all the way to the city gates, which trembled with their blows. Gilgamesh wrestled his rival to his knees with the heart of a wild man, but as in the Bible story where Jacob wrestles God, neither combatant was victorious, and the two became friends.

In the context of a lord's claim to the bride's wedding night, the combat between Gilgamesh and Enkidu reveals itself as a primitive ritual to establish who was the most powerful male, worthy of reproduction—a great stud.

The homosexual Olympic and biblical ritual

The Ancient Olympics are directly connected with the Bible through the same Sumerian accounts that Biblical myths re-work. In the *Epic of Gilgamesh*, Gilgamesh, as king, claims the right to be the first to have sex with the bride on the day of her wedding. This ancient custom was based on the idea that the king was the perfect male for procreation. But the Sumerian god began to believe that this was not correct moral conduct, and sent Enkidu to stop the king. We can understand this change in attitude to such sexual abuse, but it is harder to interpret the next move in the story.

Though Gilgamesh and Enkidu wrestled for a long time, neither was truly victorious, and they became friends. Even today, we still combatants embracing each other at the end of a bout. But Gilgamesh and Enkidu were not only friends— they also became lovers. This leads us to believe that the sacred books, were written by authors with bisexual tendencies, and that from this, the oldest literature in the world, the scribes of the Bible and of many other civilisations' myths, including the Greeks, were inspired by these depictions of homosexual love.

Ganymede—gay—Gilgamesh

Ganymede was a handsome youth, prince of the city of Troy, who was promoted to be an immortal cupbearer of the gods on Olympus. According to myth, Ganymede was kidnapped and raped by Zeus, the father of the gods.

The myth was a model for the Greek social custom of *paiderastía*, the socially acceptable erotic relationship between an adult male
and an adolescent male. The Latin form of
the name was Catamitus (and also "Ganymedes"),
from which the English word "catamite" is derived.[a]

Knowing the Olympics were organised in Zeus's honour, we must admit that there is not much moral basis
to them. The self-contradictory nature of the games will
make them seem ambiguous to some modern observers: in
one way, the ritual gave thanks for the salvation of mankind from the flood; in another, the most sacred event,
wrestling around the altar of Zeus, promoted homosexuality. Could that be the reason why women were not allowed to watch the Olympics?

---

[a]Wikipedia contributors, "Ganymede (Mythology)," *Wikipedia, The
Free Encyclopedia*, accessed 30 June 2016, https://en.wikipedia.org
/wiki/Ganymede_(mythology).

Does the Bible promote paedophilia?

The Bible can be considered in the same way as a novel, where
we look at the contents as reflecting the sexual desires of the
author. And we find nothing in the Bible against paedophilia.

The Bible was written by men, not by God himself. Therefore, what we see there in some cases is—just as in twentieth-
century works—authors explaining or interpreting phenomena

in their own way.

For example when God made woman from a rib, if we read between the lines, we could see it as genetic engineering. God extracted the life essence (DNA) of Enki from his rib's bone marrow and grafted it in the rib of Adamu. Similarly, he extracted the DNA of Ninmah from her rib's bone marrow, and grafted it into the rib of Tiamat.[9]

Like Gilgamesh, King David of Israel enjoyed the right to make a sexual claim on any of his subjects, and like Gilgamesh, David made a declaration of love to his friend—in this story, Jonathan. This love is said to have surpassed the love of a woman, and is an expression of bisexual desire.

We can also consider the Catholic Church, which throughout its history has accepted and protected hebephiles and ephebophiles (commonly referred to as "paedophiles")[10] in its ranks. Anyone who was born in a Catholic country will know a story of a pederast priest who took advantage of a young boy

---

[9] "Genetic Engineering of Humanity: DNA of the Gods—The Anunnaki Creation of Eve and the Alien Battle for Humanity," *MessageToEagle.com*, 14 November 2014, http://www.messagetoeagle.com/genetic-engineering-of-humanity-dna-of-the-gods-the-anunnaki-creation-of-eve-and-the-alien-battle-for-humanity/.

[10] "Paedophilia" properly refers to prepubescent children, whereas "ephebophilia" refers to the love of youths (generally ages fifteen to nineteen), and "hebephilia" to post-pubescent youths below fifteen. In current parlance these have tended to be conflated into "paedophilia", though in the Church sexual interest in youths has been more common than sexual interest in young children. Nevertheless, we have hereafter maintained the use of the word "paedophile" to refer also to hebephile, ephebophile, and pederast priests, as this is common in reportage today. Keeping the love of youth in mind, however, makes for a clearer link between the Church and the ancient Greeks, the men of whose aristocracy were so commonly lovers of young men.

and was transferred to another diocese to continue his "holy affairs" with other victims.

As a matter of fact, paedophilia in the Catholic Church has been a cult unto itself. Even the Polish Pope, John Paul II, disappointed us.[11] Padraic Murphy has written interesting articles on the covering up of paedophilia in the Catholic Church.[12] The response from one leading Catholic bishop has been that "he didn't think pedophile priests were aware they were committing criminal acts"[13]

As we can see, paedophilia dates back thousands of years.

Boston

The Pope's decision to appoint Cardinal Bernard Law to a prestigious Vatican post in spite of his implication in a Church child-abuse scandal showed that the paedophilia cult within the Church was stronger than the Church itself.

> Cardinal Bernard Law was appointed by the pope on Thursday to a ceremonial but highly visible post in Rome, outraging many in the archdiocese Law left in disgrace at the height of the clergy sex abuse scandal.
>
> Law, 72, will have the title of archpriest of St. Mary Major Basilica, a post often given to retired prelates.
>
> Pope John Paul II's announcement came two days after the Boston Archdiocese said it would lose at least 65

---

[11] "Post for tainted priest," *Herald Sun*, 29 May 2004.
[12] *Herald Sun* articles: 1 December 2015, "Pell was told of Evil Priests" and "Evil Priests Protected"; 2 December 2015, "Evil Priest's Sick Excuse."
[13] Lucie Morris-Marr, *Herald Sun*, 16 December 2015.

parishes as it grapples with declining collections, a shortage of priests and fallout from the scandal.

The Rev. Bob Bowers of St. Catherine's Church in Charlestown said he was astounded the Vatican would "reward" Law so soon after announcing church closings caused in part by what he considers mismanagement of the archdiocese.[14]

Perhaps the Pope was only following the holy scriptures—to which only "holy" people have access.

As far from the Olympics as this episode may seem, it does in fact help explain the meaning of the ancient games. The Olympics were a ritual connected with the Bible—a thanksgiving to the gods for the continuation of mankind and consequently for fertility. After the flood came reconciliation between gods and men; as we have already seen, this story shows why the victors in the Ancient Olympic Games were crowned with garlands of olive leaves.

Yet, the main event of the Olympics was the religious wrestling ritual held around the altar of Zeus, which promoted homosexuality. This appears to be a paradox, which contradicts the essence of the games as a ritual of fertility.

Obviously, the games existed before Aristotle, but if we read his philosophy we learn more about the full concept of the Ancient Olympics. In his book on politics, Aristotle stressed the importance of having an *autarkical* (self-sufficient) state. Athens' resources were limited, so it had to take measures to limit its population, either through abortion or by introducing homosexuality. This allows us to more fully comprehend the

---

[14] Associated Press, "Cardinal Law Appointed to Vatican Post," *Los Angeles Times*, 28 May 2004.

apparent contradiction between the games' simultaneous promotion of fertility and homosexuality: the latter was a means of controlling the birth rate and preserving the self-sufficiency and independence of the Athenian state.

We can interpret Gilgamesh's relationship with Enkidu in the same light, seeing the story of their combat on the wedding night as a means of promoting birth control against unfettered fertility.

It is hard to see homosexuality as a modern-day "disease" or even as a modern trend, if it was acceptable thousands of years ago. But it is similarly difficult to understand why homosexuality should be forbidden to the laity of the Catholic Church while pederasty has been accepted within the priesthood. Perhaps it is because the Church forbids abortions—it allows boys to be born and then has priests teach them other means of birth control according to Aristotelian motivations.

The bisexual legacy of the Ancient Olympics

The games were held to honour a god with bisexual appetites. Zeus had many female lovers and even changed into a bull to rape Europe, but he also loved young men. We can see a parallel with the bull of heaven in Sumerian mythology, and also with the amorous feelings of the gods towards young male aristocrats. In fact, the Hellenic context was one in which homosexuality was permitted and even encouraged. Gods, academics, aristocrats and warriors all practiced homosexuality. In fact, in ancient Greece the word for athlete tended to refer to a man who was forbidden to have sex with women.

Athletes were combatants who took part in the public

games of Greece, and were also young men who went through gymnastic exercises to harden themselves and become fit to bear arms. In a narrower sense, athletes were those who made the athletic or gymnastic exercises their main business, particularly wrestlers and boxers. The business of athletes was to contend at public festivals, and they regulated their habits of life accordingly. Though they were well fed, they were obliged to abstain from sex with women.

We hear from Homer that Achilles, the great hero of Troy, was deeply in love with Patroclus. Later, Alexander the Great and his male lover Hephaestion ran naked around the tomb of Achilles and Patroclus at Troy. The famous Spartan warriors cultivated not only the arts of war, but also the art of loving each other, to the point that as a people they became extinct. And it was not only the Greeks that practiced homosexuality: some Roman emperors were also homosexual.

The wrestling episode between God and Jacob in the Bible doesn't mention homosexuality, although the Biblical narratives are versions of the earlier Sumerian accounts, which had a homosexual subtext. This leads us to believe that the scribes of the Bible omitted the homosexual element in their descriptions not only of sacred wrestling, but probably many other phenomena. We must remember that the episodes in the Bible have also been modified with the changing of the times. As a result, we must rely on the Sumerian epic.

Sprinting for life

We have heard from many authors that in the beginning of the Olympics, the winner of one *stadion* or *stade* (stadium) gave his name to the Olympiad, but we have never known the reason why.

The *stadion* measured 600 feet, and at first in Olympia there wasn't even a stadium: they scratched a line on the ground and measured out the distance. Because everyone has different feet, every *stadion* had different measurements, depending on who measured it out. The winner of the *stade* was the one who was more virile, and today the expression still exists in the name *stud*, given to a sexually potent man.

The Olympics were interrupted and renewed several times. The first renewal was by Iphitus, prince of Elis (884 BC), and the second in 776 BC, from which time the Olympiads were counted. The winner of the first Olympiad was Choroebus, who gave his name to that Olympiad—but the ancient authors don't explain why. The most plausible explanation comes from James Frazer, who wrote that the ancients killed their kings to prevent them from growing old and feeble, and so every eight years, and later after every *pentaiteris*, the king had to dash for his life to prove his virility. If he lost the foot race, he would lose his kingdom and his life in favour of the more virile winner, whose name would become a symbol of the power of procreation.

According to Celtic law, a king with a disability could not be in command, and the legendary chariot race at Olympia between Pelops and King Oenomaus was also related to fertility.

Pelops and the legendary chariot race at Olympia

In the beautiful valley of Olympia, not far from Elis, there was a kingdom called Pisa, ruled by the tyrant Oenomaus, who was famous for his excellent skills in chariot racing, and also for his extreme cruelty. The king had a daughter of incomparable beauty, named Hippodamia, but due to the prediction of an oracle that he was to be murdered by his future son-in-law, he made it a condition that all the suitors for his daughter should contend with him in a chariot race, and that if he overtook them before arriving at the goal, they would die by his hand.[15]

Oenomaus had succeeded in slaying thirteen suitors—some say seventeen—by the time a young prince named Pelops, son of Tantalus, king of Lydia, arrived at Pisa and accepted the king's challenge. Lydia, whose capital was Sardis, was a fertile country in Asia Minor, and is today part of Turkey. Its people were the richest in all of Asia, and enjoyed the most luxuries. The Lydians had invented beautiful garments and costly carpets, precious ointments and exquisite foods, and a musical scale called the Lydian. They had attained a degree of civilisation long before the Greeks, and the Greek colonies in Asia Minor owed their superiority over the mother country in the arts and sciences to the Lydians. Among other things the Greeks owed to the Lydians were techniques for dying wool and melting and working ore, and the first rudiments of painting and sculpture.

Having come from such an advanced country, it was easy

---

[15] "Hippodamia," *Greek Mythology*, 19 March 2015, http://01greekmytholog y.blogspot.com.au/2015/03/hippodamia.html.

for Pelops to outsmart King Oenomaus. With a bag full of gold coins, he bribed Myrtilos, the royal charioteer, to replace the bronze axle-pins of the king's chariot with ones made of wax. The wheels stayed on only long enough for the king to get up speed, and when the wheels came off in the middle of the course, Oenomaus was catapulted from his chariot and lost his life.

Pelops, the victor, married the beautiful Hippodamia, whose name meant "horse tamer", who was deeply impressed by his courage and his beautifully toned physique. As the wife of Pelops, Hippodamia gave birth to Atreus and Thyestes. Later she committed suicide from grief at the accusation that she had misled her sons to fratricide.

Pelops gave his name to the Peloponnesus, the peninsula that comprises the southern part of Greece. After his death, Pelops received divine honours and funeral games, and a temple built for him at his grave at Olympia is still distinguishable today. East of this temple there was once another for Hippodamia, but it has disappeared.

According to Frazer in *The Golden Bough*, this story of the chariot race explains the existence of the sacred precinct of Pelops at Olympia, where the black rams, characteristic offerings to the dead, were sacrificed to the hero, and where the young men lashed themselves until blood dripped from their backs to the ground. Perhaps it also explains the high mound, at some distance from Olympia, that passed for the grave of the Hippodamia's suitors, to whose ghosts Pelops is said to have sacrificed every year.

It is possible that the men buried in this great sepulchral mound were not, as tradition had it, the suitors that contended in the chariot race for the hand of Hippodamia and, once defeated, were slain by her relentless father. They could have been men who, like Pelops himself, had won the kingdom and a bride in the chariot race and, after enjoying regal dignity and posing as living deities for some years, had finally been defeated in the race and put to death.

11. *Fire*

Poets credit the gods for fire. Its all-consuming energy, the first and most important agent of civilisation; its similarity to the sun; its intimate connection with light; its terrible and yet beneficent power; the beauty of its constantly changing flame; and its many colours and shapes all easily explain how it became an object of religious veneration, a distinguished element of mythology, and an expressive symbol in poetry, in times when cause and effect and form and essence were not yet clearly separated.

For a long time, fire was considered the presence of God on earth. In Genesis, God made a promise to Abraham; in the dark, a smoking brazier and a blazing torch, symbols of the presence of God, passed between the pieces of the sacrificed animal and Abraham realised God had made a solemn promise.[1]

---

[1] "After the sun went down, it was very dark. Suddenly a smoking firepot and a blazing torch [^Cfire and smoke often represent God] passed between the halves of the dead animals [^Lpieces; ^Ca self-curse ritual; by passing between the pieces of the sacrifice, one vowed to keep an agreement or suffer the same fate as the animals]." Gen. 15:17, The Expanded Bible.

Fire and funeral games

In the religions of the Greeks and Romans, the sepulchre was made for piety to the dead, and without it a spirit would have to wander for a hundred years. A near relative would usually catch the last breath of a dying person by opening their mouth to receive it, and then the body would be washed and crowned with flowers, and a cake of flour and honey placed in its hand as a fee for Charon.

In mythology, Charon was the son of Erebus and Nox. His office was to ferry the dead in his boat over the dark floods of the river Acheron, which is fed by the Cocytus, whose waters resound with the doleful lamentations of the dead, and also over the Styx, which is dreaded even by the immortals. Charon was usually represented as an old man with a gloomy aspect, whose beard was matted and garments tattered. Those who could not pay the fare, or who had found no grave in the upper world, were compelled to wander on the desolate banks of the Acheron until Charon was pleased to carry them over to their final resting place.

This practice of payment respected the origin of the fable in the mythology of Egypt, where if a dead person stood unaccused of any crime, or if any accusations were found groundless, the judges would decree regular burial and eulogies were pronounced to the applause of bystanders. Their talents, virtues and accomplishments—everything but their rank and riches—were praised. To carry the corpse to the cemetery, it was necessary to cross the lake and pay a small sum for the passage.

This circumstance was also transplanted into Greek mythology. The cemetery was a large plain, surrounded by trees and intersected by canals, and was called Elisout or Elisiaens, meaning rest. Most readers will recognise, in these myths, the ferryman Charon, the coin for payment, and the Elysian fields.

The whole ceremony of interment, for the Greeks, seems to have consisted in depositing the deceased in an excavation made in the rock or under the sand that covered the whole Elisout; it seems that then the relations of the deceased threw three handfuls of sand as a sign to the workmen to fill up the cavity, after saying three loud farewells.

Elysium or the Elysian fields

Elysium was the name given to certain regions that the ancients supposed to be the residence of the blessed after death. It is sometimes described as consisting of delightful meadows, and at other times of islands at the western edges of the earth. The happiness of the blessed was a life of tranquil enjoyment, and the images of that happiness were taken partly from myths of Olympus and partly from descriptions of the golden age. Beautiful meadows alternated with pleasant groves, over which a serene and cloudless sky spread. A soft, celestial light shed magical brilliance over every object.

In Elysium, the heroes renewed their favourite sports. They exercised in wrestling and other contests, danced to the sound of the lyre, or wandered—sometimes alone and sometimes in company—through scented laurel groves on the smiling banks of the Eridanus and in delightful vales, or in meadows watered by limpid fountains, amid the warbling of birds. A perpetual spring reigned there. The voluptuous description of the gardens of Armida in the poet Torquato Tasso's *Jerusalem De-*

livered imitates these ancient ideas of the Elysian fields. The Parisians have called one of their favourite gardens and places of amusement the *Champs-Élysées* (Elysian fields).

Burial and burning

The ancient Greeks practiced burial and cremation indifferently. In burial, the body was placed with the face upward and the head towards the west. Pyres for burning varied in form and in the materials used, but were lit by the closest relative before perfumes and wine were poured upon them. The dead person was typically burned in their richest clothes. After burning, the ashes of the dead were collected and deposited in an urn. These traditions applied not only to the Greeks, but also to the Romans and Celts, whose rites were almost identical.

The practice of burning by night explains the origin of the word *funeral*, which comes from *funes* (torches). In Portuguese, *fumaca* is smoke and the verb *fumare* is "to smoke".

Eulogies were often delivered at the funerals of distinguished men, and funeral games were held in honour of the dead. In Europe, the practice of burning was discontinued until the close of the fourth century. The wake, or watching, is still celebrated today, and burial feasts are still held in more remote districts. The Irish can tell us that the wake, in some parts of their country, can be a scene of tumult and drunkenness. In Lisbon, on the way to the cemetery of the Lumiar, there is a restaurant called *A volta ca te espero* (We Are Waiting for You on the Way Back), suggesting, in a subtle manner, that the staff are ready to feast mourners lavishly on their way back from the cemetery.

Funeral words

Lumiar From *lume* (fire) and *ar* (air). Lumiar is a Biblical allegory of the gods' presence.

Cemetery From the Latin *cemeterium* (burial place) and the Greek *koimeterion,* meaning first "sleeping place" and later "burial place."

Koi Portuguese—also *coi.* Hiding place.

It is curious to note that the Celtic Druids used to say that heroes never die, but are only asleep, and mingling Greek and Celtic mythology with the help of the Portuguese language we can say that a cemetery is a hiding place along with a sleeping or burying place.

The famous burial site of the ancient Egyptians was situated beyond Lake Acherusia or Acharejish, whose name signified the last condition of time and which is probably the foundation of the Greek fables of Lake Acheron. On the banks of Lake Acherusia, a tribunal of forty-two judges inquired into the life and character of the deceased; a corpse could not be carried to the cemetery beyond the lake before undergoing this inquisition. If the deceased had died insolvent, the court assigned the corpse to his creditors, to oblige his relations and friends to pay his debts. If his life had been wicked, they refused his body the privilege of solemn burial and had it carried out and thrown into a large ditch made for such shameful disposal. This ditch had the name Tatar, because of the lamentations this sentence produced in surviving friends and relations. The Greek hell,

Tatarus, had its origin in this Egyptian Tartar.

Funeral games

The most famous games of Europe all developed from funeral games, and those of the Golden Circuit were no exception. The Olympics arose from the funeral games of King Oenomaus, the Isthmian from games in honour of Palaemon or Melicerta. The Nemean Games originated from funeral games in honour of Opheltes or Archemorus, or, in another account, by Heracles after he had killed the Nemean Lion. The Pythian Games commemorated Apollo's killing the serpent Python. The Lughnasadh games were instituted by Lugh on the spot where his foster mother was buried, and the Capitoline Games gained their name from the head (*caput*) of the hero Tollius.

Our analysis brings us to the conclusion that the rituals were funeral rites and also attempts to ensure a good crop. The Palaemon who became Melicerta and the Opheltes who became Archemorus are like the Celtic hag who turned into a beautiful woman, representing the fertilisation of the land. The traditional sacrifice of a head, either of a human or a horse, is a tradition of the Indo-European family: Romans and Celts alike used to offer the head of a champion horse and used the blood for the lustral sacrifices.

In the film *The Godfather*, the capos (short for *caporegime*) are the boss's generals: the *heads* that command his front-line operatives. In one of the film's most well-known scenes, mafiosi place a champion horse's head on its owner's pillow as an act of revenge and intimidation. But in ancient times, to burn a champion horse on an altar was a sacrifice of thanksgiving

to ensure the return of the sun and the continuation of fertility. Showing a rich capacity for invention, the ancients conceived the notion that the sun, which appeared every day from
the east, ascended the sky dressed in red and driving a golden
chariot pulled by two flaming horses. This explains the sacrifice of the champion's head, to ensure that the flaming horses
would continue to bring the sun back every day.

Funeral rites

Funeral games at the graves of important people were prevalent among the ancients. Why did they, our ancestors, organise
games to commemorate the dead?

It is not always easy to determine why one nation decided
to preserve corpses through arduous and expensive processes,
as did the Egyptians, while another decided to burn it and another still to bury it. Religious beliefs and material conditions
helped to decide how friends and relatives would pay their last
tribute to the remains of the dead. Yet, in *The Golden Bough*,
Frazer manages to give us a comprehensive interpretation of
funeral games.

What Frazer says tends to support the traditional explanation of the great Irish fairs, which were held at the beginning of
August, when the first corn is ripe, and tended to take place at
the burial grounds of kings and other famous people. The horse
races and other games that formed the most prominent feature
of the celebrations were, it is said, instituted in honour of these
dead men and women, and were also intended to ensure a plentiful harvest and an abundance of fruit and fish. So long as the
spirits of these dead, who were buried at the site of the celeb-

ration, received the homage of their descendants in the form of funeral games and, perhaps, an offering of the first fruits of the harvest, it was supposed that they would continue to bless the people by causing the earth to bring forth its fruits, the cows to yield their milk, and the waters to swarm with fish. To imagine the importance that the funerals of famous people must have had in antiquity, we can remember the death of Princess Diana, whose funeral and burial was one of the biggest media events of the late twentieth century and represented a modern revival of the funeral festivals.

European burying-grounds afford the finest views

There has long been a romantic sentimentalism regarding the dead, which new generations still display. In France, cemeteries are tourist attractions. The most prestigious of these, the Cimetière du Père Lachaise, is situated on the highest hill in the eastern part of Paris, and was bought by Napoleon, who created the reserve in 1803. King Louis XIV had a country house built there for his confessor, François de la Chaise, and its extensive garden is now called "the city of the dead."

The celebrated burying place occupies a very considerable space, and contains a great variety of tombs, columns, obelisks, pyramids, funeral vases, and monuments of all kinds, and is covered with flowers. There lie Molière, La Fontaine, Oscar Wilde, Frederic Chopin, Edith Piaf, and General Maximilien Foy, amid a crowd of philosophers, artists, warriors, politicians, and ordinary people. From the cemetery, you look down on one

of the most beautiful and interesting spots in the world. Another Paris cemetery, the Cimetière Montmartre, became the
model on which European cemeteries are constructed. In Lisbon, all cemeteries are situated on hills where spirits can look
over sea and land from on high.

The reason that cemeteries were located in these lofty
places was because thanksgiving rituals were considered food
for the gods and always took place at high elevations, surrounded by beautiful panoramas. As a chef adorns a plate to make
the food more beautiful, so the sacrifices to the gods were performed in the midst of a picture where all of nature was visible
from a single point.

Lampadephoroi or lampadedromia: The relay or torch race

The famous relay or torch races took place in Athens at the
Vulcanalia, Promethia, Panathenaea, and other festivals. The
runners were youths, and it was decided by lot who should
have the privilege of beginning the race. The one who did so, if
his torch was extinguished before he reached the goal, handed
it to the second competitor, who gave it to a third should it be
extinguished again. Poets often used the delivery of the torch
from one runner to another as an image in their work.

He who succeeded in carrying the burning torch to the goal
was declared the victor. If a runner went too slowly, to avoid
extinguishing his torch, spectators in this race would drive him
on by beating him with their open hands.

The torch race (*torch* comes from the Latin *tortus* (to twist), because the torch was made of a twisted roll of tough wool and other materials) took place from the altar of Prometheus and the Academy of Plato, and finished in the Acropolis after a distance of approximately 2,500 metres. In this race, where all twelve districts of the city were represented, it is said that runners often only made it a distance of 60 metres. The race was organised by the *gymnasiarch*, who selected the best youths to compete from the gymnasiums around the city.

The Panathenaea festival

The festival of Panathenaea was celebrated at Athens in honour of the tutelary deity Minerva. Ericthonius, who may have instituted the festival though others say Orpheus was the founder, called it Athenaea, but when Theseus united the inhabitants of the twelve districts into a city, the festival received the name *Pan*athenaea (*pan* meaning *universal*) because it was thereafter solemnised by all the tribes of Athens.

The Panathenaea was conducted by ten presidents, known as Athlothetae. On its first day, there were torch races; on the second, gymnastic exercises; on the third, contests of music and declamation and dramatic representations. In later times, imitations of naval battles were introduced. An olive crown from the groves of the academies, and a vessel full of the finest olive oil, were the rewards of the victor. After the games followed sacrifices and a sacrificial feast.

The greater Panathenaea were distinguished not only by their greater splendour and longer duration, but also by the solemn procession in which the Peplus, a sacred garment consecrated by young virgins, made of white wool and adorned with gold embroidery representing the battle of the giants, was carried from the Acropolis into the temple of the goddess, where it covered her ivory statue. The Peplus was also used in the Panathenaea as the sail of a ship that moved through the streets by way of secret machinery and which was followed by a solemn procession.

This festival was so holy that criminals were released from prisons on the occasion of its celebration, and gold crowns were conferred on men of distinguished merit.

Prometheus

Prometheus, the god of fire, was a son of Japetus and Clymene (a daughter of Oceanus) and the father of Deucalion. Cunning and expedient, he opposed Zeus, founder of the new race of gods, whom he had at first supported. When some of the Titans proposed to expel Cronus from the throne and elevate his son Zeus in his place, Prometheus had advised them to work by cunning, as Themis and Earth had revealed to him that wits, and not force, would give them victory.

The Titans ignored Prometheus's advice and with it the chance to win against Cronus. Zeus, who despised poor mortals, determined to extinguish them and create a new race. But Prometheus thwarted him by secretly bestowing on men the fire that Zeus had concealed. To punish this offence, Zeus sent Pandora to bring all manner of diseases into the world, and had Prometheus chained by Hephaestus on a rock of the Caucasus, which to the earlier Greeks was considered the eastern edge of the world.

Prometheus suffered his torment with heroic firmness, and

told his son Deucalion to build an ark. These two traditions, of a rebellion against the gods and the building of an ark to protect humanity from a flood of divine origin, are united in the story of Prometheus by Aeschylus, while Hesiod relates the cause of Zeus's anger at mortals.

The gods once attempted, at Mecone, to make an agreement with men determining what honours the gods should enjoy and what duties men owed them for their protection. Prometheus appeared on behalf of men, making the case that the gods should not impose duties that were too burdensome upon them.

Prometheus brought a bull as an offering, from which the gods were to select a portion for their share. After the animal was cut up, Prometheus divided the pieces into two heaps: in one the flesh and fat entrails, wrapped in the skin and covered with the stomach; and in the other the bones, artfully concealed in the fat. Zeus failed to see through the trick and chose the fat, but became indignant on finding that the portion contained only bones. Hesiod writes that from then on it became the custom to offer the gods bones without flesh.

In Lucian's *Dialogues*, Prometheus is not only accused of dividing the flesh of the sacrifice in this way, and of stealing fire, but is also credited with creating man. According to Apollodorus, he formed man of clay and water and bestowed fire on him by kindling dry wood in the sun.

Plato's version of the story is that the gods made the animals from earth and fire, but left Prometheus and his brother Epimetheus to arrange the proportions in which these materials should be assigned to each species. Epimetheus distributed the best powers among the rational animals, and Prometheus, wanting not to leave man altogether helpless, obtained the arts of fire for them by stealth, from Hephaestus and Athena.

Other poets and philosophers have modified these myths according to their particular objectives. As the god of fire, the pagan Greek Prometheus showed more benevolence to men than did Jehovah, the god of fire in the Biblical scriptures. In Exodus, we are told that Moses had lived many years as a herdsman when one day he saw a bright light in the desert. He advanced near it and was excited to hear a voice coming from the flames he found. "I am Jehovah," said the voice. "I have heard the lamentations of my people undergoing punishment in Egypt. I am sending you to free them and bring them back to their own land of Canaan."

In this episode, we see a similar mythology to the story of Prometheus, where the subject, a god, is described as resembling fire. But in the Greek myth, the god of fire saved the entire human race, while in the Bible, God only saved the tribe of the Hebrews. In the Greek context, we can see the torch relay race as another thanksgiving ritual offered to the god of fire for the salvation of mankind.

Hieromenia: The sacred truce

The olive branch, celebrated in the mythology of the Celts, Greeks, and Romans, was revered and considered the symbol of peace and humility. For more than a thousand years, all wars ceased for the duration of the ancient games, to allow people to travel to and from the festivals. Any person or city breaking the truce was disqualified from participating in the games, and at Delphi, site of the Pythian Games, they were also banned from consulting the famous Oracle of Apollo.

Yet, the truce seems to us more a matter of romance than reality, and in some ways a fiction of the poets. We know, in fact, that wars occurred many times during the games, and even interrupted the pentathlon. The city of Sparta was fined for violating the Olympic peace during the Peloponnesian War. The Greek city of Pisa, near Olympia, tried in 364 BC to regain its initial control of the games by taking possession of the Altis by force, but its soldiers were thwarted and expelled by a force of Elians and Spartans.

Why was the truce imposed so strictly?

Knowing the sacred truce was a thanksgiving ritual intended to please the sun god and ensure the continuation of fertility, we can see why the Greeks, Celts, and Romans imposed the death penalty on trucebreakers. The suspension of hostilities by agreement, during the games, allowed time for atonement and reconciliation—a further reason that it was necessary to castigate those who violated or disturbed the peace. Peacebreakers were seen not only to be disturbing public harmony but also the accord between gods and men, thus endangering the land's continued fertility.

Why were women not allowed to watch or compete in the Olympics?

Women's exclusion from the Olympics was a severe act of retaliation against Pandora, the first woman, for being the cause of men having to endure intensive labour and fatigue. According to Greek mythology, Pandora is the counterpart of the biblical Eve, who caused God to expel man from paradise.

Paradise was a garden—the Garden of Eden—where the first ancestors of the human race were placed after the creation, to live in a state of innocence before they forfeited God's favour and were expelled for their disobedience.

Pandora

The first woman created by the Greek gods, Pandora ("the all-gifted") was so named because she received gifts from all the gods of Olympus. Prometheus, whom Zeus had driven from Olympus, formed man and animated him with fire stolen from heaven. Zeus, indignant and determined to punish the offence, commanded Hephaestus to fashion a woman of clay, equal to a goddess in beauty and grace, and to give her life and the power of speech.

According to other accounts, Pandora was the creature of Prometheus, whom the gods came down to see and bestow their gifts upon. In this story, Minerva instructed her in all works of female skill; Aphrodite endowed her with beauty and fascination; and Hermes instilled in her the desire to please, and taught her insinuating words. Zeus presented her with a vase or chest that contained all human woes, then sent Hermes to Epimetheus, Prometheus's brother, with Pandora and the fatal gift.

Prometheus had warned Epimetheus not to accept any of Zeus's gifts, but the charms of the virgin Pandora overcame his caution. Until that time, man had lived free from evil, oppressive labour, and disease. But Pandora brought with her a whole list of calamities that rushed out and spread across the world when Epimetheus (or some say Pandora) raised the lid of her box out of curiosity, an act that had been forbidden by divine command. Only hope remained at the bottom of the chest, which the rash opener swiftly closed, and hope alone allows man to endure his miseries and hardships.

Even though the myth of Pandora is now an ancient one, the Catholic Church to this day perpetuates the idea that women are to blame for the existence of sin and death, and the Church continues to appeal to biblical myths to maintain the political subjection of women. Though as a child I would go to church, and was brought up a Catholic, I am no longer so willing to attend and believe. Women were the biggest losers in the advent of Christianity, which we can see when we compare the dogmatic authoritarianism of Christianity with the democracy of ancient Celtic society.

Christianity made women into second-class citizens. According to the Celtic mentality, the source of life is integrally associated with both women and men. This is contrary to the view of the Catholic Church, which teaches that women are inferior. The Bible is like a manual for learning how to criticise and degrade women. It is seemingly impossible to understand how some men can hate women so much.

The Church defends women's suffering in childbirth—a cruel sentiment towards women who are giving birth, an act that is the essence of the sacred circle of life. My father always reminds me of my grandmother who, he still refers to as a great goddess, even though she has passed away into the other world. In Celtic mythology, women were warriors and goddesses, and this consciousness should live on today. I view my own mother in this way, as a powerful woman who I stand by and always look up to.

I feel displeased with the Biblical and mythological accounts that say all calamities rushed out and spread across the world because of women. During the Inquisition, the ghastly spectre of such myths formed an excuse to torture and burn women alive, on the basis that men's misfortunes, miseries, and hardships have their root in Adam's temptation by Eve.[2] When investigating the Bible, I realised that such nonsense must have been the invention of crafty scribes with homosexual inclinations. The same ones who created the Biblical stories of wrestling rituals, with their homoerotic overtones, must have also created the Eve myth. From then until now, the Bible has been an instrument used by paedophile priests against innocent boys, and their abuse has been carefully obscured by the Church's protection and cover-ups.

---

[2] Those wanting to learn more about the role and treatment of women in the Bible should refer to Barbara G. Walker, *Belief and Unbelief: Womanhood Beyond Religion* (Washington: Humanist Press, 2014). Kindle edition.

12. The State Library of Victoria: A sacred place

The State Library of Victoria is a sacred place of culture and a temple of knowledge. Looking at its magnificent Corinthian-inspired architecture, we should feel fortunate that our Victorian temple did not suffer a fate like that of the Library of Alexandria, which was gutted in 391 AD by a frenzied crowd of Christians at the instigation of the fanatical pope Theophilus and its treasures destroyed or scattered. The historian Osoris relates that at the beginning of the fifth century, only empty shelves were to be seen in the library. The Victorian temple, by contrast, is still not only a magnificent edifice, but is also filled with seemingly infinite knowledge whose contents can throw light on the fortunate rise of Australian democracy.

The controversy over Australia's first settlers

Among Australians of a few generations ago, there is a sense of shame that their ancestors were convicts deported from Britain. It drives us to ask the logical question, "How could this beautiful country, which leads the world in many fields, have risen from a foundation of thieves, robbers, and murderers?"

Professor Manning Clark gives one of the great accounts of

the early years of European settlement in Australia in his distinctive interpretation of Australian history.[1] Contemporaries judged the convicts according to their political opinions, and their opponents spoke and wrote of them as men who propagated the supposedly monstrous doctrine of the rights of man. Supposedly, they seduced the weak and ignorant who were susceptible to such persuasion to believe that they should overturn government, law, property, security, religion, order, and everything else that was valuable in their country. So, to protect the ignorant against such delusions they agreed to have them removed to a place where they could do no further harm—Australia. The convicts' supporters, on the other hand, offered them the consolation enjoyed by all martyrs in the cause of liberty.

Law

Justice is often represented by a woman holding a scale and a sword. In British courts during the beginnings of Australian settlement, the beam of the scale (the sword) always leaned towards the rich plate: they favoured the aristocrats and the bourgeois.

---

[1] Manning Clark, *A History of Australia, Volumes I & II: From the Earliest Times to 1838* (Melbourne: Melbourne University Press, 1995). These volumes deal with the era before white settlement and the earliest years of European colonisation, through to the establishment of an increasingly settled society and the expeditions of the great inland explorers. This is not a general Australian history—it does not attempt to cover all aspects—and it is not a definitive or quantitative analysis. It is, rather, a work of art: a living and breathing account of the remaking of a primitive continent. It is history come alive.

During the colonial period, trial by jury in the courts of England and France was also of doubtful merit. In England, one had to have a certain income to be a juror, and the same applied in France, where attention was also paid to circumstances of rank. Jurors, who were mainly men of business from the middle classes, tended to be hostile to thieves, swindlers, or worse, and had no hesitation in condemning the accused to deportation. Part of the reason for this was that many times such convicts were used as free labourers on properties the bourgeois owned overseas.

In Portugal, during the period of its colonial empire, judges were even more severe than the law demanded. Their ignorance and carelessness caused mistakes and abuses that their pride and the clannish spirit of the upper classes prevented from being rectified. Under their watch, whole crowds of innocent people lost liberty, property, reputation, and even life.

But the revolution of 25 April 1974 showed how legislative caprice cannot, in the end, prevail over the irresistible influence of public opinion. In the days following that democratic revolution, the jails of Portugal opened their doors to release the political prisoners, and repopulated the cells with political police. No legislator can escape that invisible power of the masses, the often silent judgment that tends eventually to correct the mistakes of arbitrary government and see the people's rights defended.

António Salazar, the prime minister of the authoritarian Portuguese state for thirty-six years, gave orders to the political police to kill Humberto Delgado, a general of the Portuguese air force, who had previously been robbed of a victory in an unfairly-run presidential election. Delgado had promised the Portuguese people that if he won, he would dismiss the dictator. When Delgado was assassinated in Spain, his family decided to open an inquiry and engaged one of the best Portuguese lawyers to prosecute this political murder case—not an easy task, as the country was ruled at the time by the secret police, the *Policia Internacional e de Defensa do Estado* (PIDE; International and State Defence Police). Nevertheless, one lawyer, Dr Mario Soares, a man of culture and courage, accepted the case and tried to challenge the fascists' laws. Because of that, he was deported to Saõ Tomé, a former Portuguese colony.

After the revolution of 1974, Dr Soares became the leader of the Portuguese Socialist Party and prime minister of Portugal, and twice in a row was elected president of the republic. These extraordinary events of only a few decades ago can help us understand the predicament of many of the convicts who were deported to Australia.

Patriotism and the law are both ambiguous

Generally, we believe that the law exists to protect the innocent and punish the guilty. But when accusations are made of political crimes, the government has a strong motive to produce a conviction, irrespective of the truth or whether a sentence would constitute any kind of justice. Such arbitrary exercise of power created the large crowds of first settlers, who came to Australia. They were not criminals but martyrs of patriotism and, in fact, were often Celts—the guardians of liberty.

Among one group of Celtic convicts there were five Scottish martyrs: Muir, Palmer, Margaret, Skiving and Gerald. In December 1792, Thomas Muir, a legal advocate, presented an address from the United Irishmen in Dublin to a convention in Edinburgh, which recommended fundamental changes in the political system. For this he was tried at Edinburgh and sentenced to transportation for fourteen years. In 1793 the Reverend Thomas Fyshe Palmer transcribed and circulated the pamphlet 'An address to the people'—for which he was transported for five years. In November 1793 Skiving, Gerald and Margaret were sentenced to transportation for fourteen years for the opinions they had expressed at the Edinburgh convention on political reform.[2]

The sacrifices of these Celtic martyrs deported to Australia, both men and women, were not in vain. The sword of the Celtic goddess of war, Scátach, mother of heroes (Sacha in Portuguese) descended to us in the form of Australian laws that protect the working class and make it a paradise for labour, despite the ferocity of capitalist forces. Australian law and lawgivers, along with judges, lawyers, and unions, are leading the world in the fields of wages, industrial relations, health and safety, workplaces and so on. In other words, these laws protect the rights of the working class against the sharp sword of capitalism.

Welcome to the wonderful country of Celtic law. Why do more than 146 nationalities call Australia home? Because the rights and privileges of the people were asserted within its laws, which have a basis in Celtic culture.

---

[2]Ben Wilkie, "Radicals, Martyrs, and Scottish Convicts in Colonial Australia," *History of the Scots in Australia*, 25 August 2015, https://thescottishaustralian.wordpress.com/2015/08/25/radicals-martyrs-and-scottish-convicts-in-colonial-australia/.

Should cultural crimes be punished by the law?

If I am to ask whether cultural crimes should be punished by the law, I should perhaps leave the reply to parents who are paying bills and students and lawgivers who hope that in due course, judges will have the power to prosecute those who falsify history and corrupt the ideals of science. In a court, if the prosecution proved that a policeman had lied to save a criminal, the judge would condemn that policeman for deceiving the court and failing in his ethical duty.

Statistics show that a majority of the Australian population traces its ancestry back to the Celts. So, why don't Australian schools teach Celtic history? In Australia, politicians go to jail when they defraud the system. In democracy the law is impartial to all citizens.

Why are historians who misrepresent history allowed to go unpunished? Academic obstinacy, in not exposing the Olympic truth, that the ancient games were part of a larger and older tradition, is a cultural crime. Perniciously, many historians around the world, teaching at prestigious universities, continue to present the ancient Olympic festival as solely the tradition of the ancient Greeks. As though in an obstinate religious fervour, or perhaps out of political self-interest, they deny the truth of history for the purpose of avoiding knowledge. They refuse to teach that the Ancient Olympics, as a religious, cultural, and sporting ritual, was embraced by many ancient nations. This solemn entertainment was the product of traditions common to numerous ethnic communities, making it equivalent to the modern universal sporting religion, soccer.

I myself have encountered this refusal while studying an archaeology and anthropology degree: the main subjects offered covered only Greek, Egyptian, and Roman history. If you are a descendant of the Celts, and thus part of the largest ethnic group in Australia, you may ask why there is a total lack of subjects on Celtic history, and on the Celtic culture that dominated Europe long before Romanisation and still does today.

Everyone who speaks on matters connected to their profession should be sure of what they are talking about. Yet, it seems that historians around the world often believe that what they learned up to their graduation is enough to sustain an academic career. However, we know that these days, continued learning is essential: one must not lose sight of the train of modern technology or the advance of human knowledge. Not one profession can afford to ignore innovation, at the risk of affecting their trade. This applies to doctors, engineers, and carpenters, and practitioners of every trade in between.

Policemen need absolute determination and fearlessness to fulfil their duties. Surgeons must have courage to perform their operations. Minors, too, must be brave. Paratroopers need undaunted spirit to jump from an aircraft. Teachers also need the qualities of mind that allow human beings to encounter danger and difficulty without fear. In this respect, my father has learned through his experience, suffering the censorship imposed by the fascists during the regime of the dictator Salazar. While he was a student, attending Portuguese academic institutions, the beliefs of intellectuals were restricted to what the supreme leader, Salazar, suggested to the popular mind. Such alienation from one's own capacity to think occurred under the scrupulous supervision of the secret police, who refused to accept the gag imposed by their country's sick regime.

Today, my father tells me that he understands now why his teachers were horrified any time a student asked an impertinent question, such as "Why the colonial war?", "Why censorship?", and "Why doesn't the Church raise its voice against fascism?" His teachers always replied by saying that these matters were irrelevant and did not concern students. Their reluctance to answer extended even to questions about Portuguese history. My father's great interest in this subject compelled him to contest some obvious lies when teachers tried to throw salt water ("holy water") in his eyes, saying that the main objective of Portuguese maritime expansion was the propagation of Christianity.

Portuguese expeditions

In the sixteenth and seventeenth centuries, Portugal and Spain launched several expeditions to what was then known as *Terra Australis* (Southern Land). They lost interest when they found little of value for European trade. Later, the Dutch developed a sound knowledge of the new continent, calling it New Holland. But they, too, gave up their interest, opening the way for the arrival of the English captain James Cook.

At school, my father was taught the reason behind such expeditions around the world was to spread the Catholic faith. However, the reality behind any expedition was always to find trading opportunities—spices in Malaysia, porcelain in China and Japan, and so on. But when the Portuguese arrived in the Pilbara they didn't see a trading opportunity therefore they left, with no thought of spreading the faith there. The fleet then "evidently went as far as rounding Wilson's Promontory (named *Cabo Formoza*, meaning "Cape Beautiful") and sailed along the south coast as far as Kangaroo Island, off present-day Adelaide before turning back,"[3] again apparently without thought of the souls in that land that might have been saved.

This sequence of events shows that the Portuguese holy argument, fabricated by the Catholic Church, has no authenticity.

Another issue that my father raises is that he cannot understand why the Inquisition had to burn people alive in Lisbon, with the intention of confiscating their property, given that the majority of the people burned were Jews and that Jesus Christ himself was Jewish.

A paradoxical history

The rest of the world tends to consider Australia a country with only a little more than two hundred years of civilisation. But we can show some leadership when it comes to teaching history.

For example, when scientists wanted to learn about prehistoric rock-painting techniques, they came to Australia to acquire knowledge from Aboriginal artists who are still using skills from the Palaeolithic era. And when Dutch technicians wanted to build a replica of their historical ship, the *Batavia*, which was lost in Australian waters in the seventeenth century, they had to visit the Perth museum that displays that shipwreck's remains.

---

[3]Peter Trickett, "Wrong Turn over the First Maps of Australia's Coasts," *Canberra Times*, 18 January 2014, http://www.canberratimes.com.au/act-news/wrong-turn-over-the-first-maps-of-australias-coasts-20140117-31ore.html.

More recently, my father, a Portuguese freelance historian, also searched Australian libraries for clues that could guide him to the fabulous civilisation of his ancestors, the Celtiberians, and also to the mystical folklore of the most important games of ancient Europe, including the Ancient Olympics.

The largest part of the Australian population traces its ancestry to Great Britain, Ireland, and the rest of Europe. My father firmly believes that Australian historians have a cultural and moral obligation to teach this population—whether they trace their ancestry from Britain, Portugal, or Poland—that their ancestors held a more important games festival than the Ancient Olympics of the Greeks.

Many history books teach that anthropologists believe the Aboriginal people migrated from South East Asia at least 40,000 years ago. But the story given by Aboriginal folklore claims that Australia's indigenous people were always there. More recently, scientists have told us there is evidence that the Aborigines have been in Australia for more than 175,000 years, and I am optimistic—having studied the Aboriginal stream in Australian archaeology—that as we advance in our technology we will uncover still further evidence.

The paradoxical academicism of Portuguese scholars

Portugal inherited its territory from the ancient Lusitanians, a Celtic tribe. However, at the beginning of the twenty-first century, the universities of Portugal still keep the Portuguese uninformed about their Celtic inheritance, or at least its culture.

At the foundation of the Portuguese nation, the politicians used the Lusitanian culture to defend the division of Portuguese territory, belonging to the Portuguese people, from Spain.

We can consider Portugal as the oldest European country, on the basis that its frontiers have not changed since 1245. And the academics of my father's country have a strong moral obligation to teach the Portuguese the sacred culture of the people from whom they inherited their land and folklore—my ancestors, the Celts. But the only thing my father was able to learn was that he is Lusitanian, or Lusitano (m.) or Lusitana (f.), as they would say in Portugal.

I am Lusa-Australiana and my brother is Luso-English, names that mixing our cultural heritage with the countries where we were born. It is interesting to note that academics wouldn't refer to me as *Portuguesa-Australiana*, but as Lusa-Australiana.[4] But if a Lusa or Luso wants to enquire about Lusitanian history, the information is very scarce. In Portugal one rarely finds references to it, and even that is distorted in an attempt to obscure the truth.

Thanks to destiny, my father came to Australia, where he not only learned about the fabulous culture of his ancestors but also found out why Portuguese academics had distorted its history.

---

[4] Academics explain that the term Lusa–Australiana is correctly constructed according to the rules of an agglutinative language. However my father has taught me the true reason for using this term: the formal name for Portugal was Lusitania—which refers to Lugh or Lugo, the sun god, and Ania, the moon. The name *Lusitanians*, then, refers to the warriors or people of light in Celtic mythology.

A love of history is a great cultural gift

The classical era of Greek history displayed a refined appreciation of the arts, but to neglect Celtic history in its favour is a cultural crime. Some historians, to cover their ignorance of Celtic history, even argue that the Celts never existed. And despite the fact that a majority of Australians are of Celtic origin, Australian schools don't teach Celtic history—ironic, since most Australian teachers could also trace their ancestry back to the Celts.

I hope this Chariot of Knowledge will help to start a race to catch up on one of the great civilisations of the freeborn. Celts were the inventors of social and political liberty. The Celtic torc, an open ring around the neck, is the symbol of the free man, contrasting with the closed and locked steel collar of the slave. All the great civilisations but the Celts had slaves.

The archaeological museum in Lisbon contains the world's best collection of Celtic torcs. But no one explains to the visitors that the torc is not only a beautiful ornament but is above all a symbol of freedom. And ironically, that fantastic museum is also the repository of many rare pieces collected during the great epoch of the Portuguese navigators, who inaugurated an era of colonialism and subjugation. Unfortunately, despite Portugal's strong Celtic heritage, which steeped it in a love of freedom, in the sixteenth century, new rules made under the guidance of the Catholic Church allowed Portuguese seafarers to trade in slaves. The Portuguese argued that Africans had no soul, so to buy and sell black people wasn't a sin. The Vatican agreed and endorsed the argument in exchange for a tax payment.

The people hadn't changed—what had changed was their

education. In the glorious times of the Celtic civilisation, people learned to respect the liberty of others. In the sixteenth century, under the new light of that great and invisible God whose existence the heathens had but glimmerings of, the Portuguese people were allowed to trade slaves so long as they lined the pockets of the priests.

Celtic ancestry and the festival of the three Fs

How is my father both Celtic and Portuguese? I am often asked. Even Celts from Ireland have asked this. Few today seem aware of Portugal's Lusitanian heritage. And to these sceptical questioners I must say that my father's fervour for Celtic history has no frontiers. In fact, my father is the only one in Portugal who I know to write and sing Celtic *fados*.

The *fado* is the Portuguese national song; the chorus that was performed at the ancients' sacrifices of the goat. The fandango is the dance performed on the banks of rivers during the ritual of fertility related to the motherland, and the sacrifice of the pig. And the *faena* (bullfight) is the ritual of fertility related to the sun god and the sacrifice of the bull.

Though Portugal was Romanised two thousand years ago, it is still the only country to maintain the festival of the three Fs.

Celts, Greeks, Jews, and Arabs used to live in harmony until religious conflicts forced them apart. Millions of Celts who have been dispersed around the globe. In the United States alone, there are about 45 million people of Irish descent. In fact, if we could scrutinise the whole population of the United

States, we would find that the majority traced their ancestry to the Celts.

I hope this Chariot of Knowledge will not only open the doors of public libraries, but also the doors of universities. In the United States, there are historians who say that even some American Indians are descendants of the Celts. Apparently, there is evidence that Celts arrived in America before the birth of Christ, sailing from Spain.[5] More than two thousand years ago, the Celts had better boats than the caravels of Columbus. Apparently, they could transport up to two hundred people, compared to the eighty that Columbus carried, and their sails were much stronger, having been made of cow's skins sewn together. But that is a story for another chariot—or another boat.

Celtic fate

Celtic history is full of martyrs. What was once a powerful civilisation now still awaits its proper recognition in the history books. I can understand that two thousand years ago, the enemies of the Celts wanted to destroy their philosophers, poets, artists, warriors, and everybody who defended the rights of man. It is harder to understand why today, many historians of Celtic ancestry are alienating themselves from their heritage.

The Celts must regain lost knowledge, but how is this possible if, over the centuries, their enemies have destroyed their philosophers? The answer lies in ancestral wisdom. Though today's Celts to not have their elders to teach them, according

[5]Barry Fell, *America B.C.: Ancient Settlers in the New World, Revised Edition* (Pocket, 1989).

to Celtic wisdom, heroes never die—they are only asleep. Communication can be had with departed spirits by those whose minds are set on spiritual things.

My father believes that, long after it has quit the body, the immortal part of man, the spirit, can animate those persons inspired by the divine. To achieve such a communion needs endurance of mind and body, which can be attained by watching less television, doing more exercise, and meditating. We must be persistent and have patience and constancy, he says, to exert the habits of mind that let us listen to the ancestors, and we desperately need the intensity of feeling that warms the breasts of Celtic mothers who feed the bodies and souls of successive generations.

Until the arrival of Latin prose, Celtic poetry was the guardian of all knowledge

Celtic traditions were not committed to writing. When the Romans introduced Latin literacy, writing belonged to the Catholic priests, whose exclusive protection of this knowledge made them guides of men in science and the arts, as well as in religion. Celtic knowledge was absorbed from Latin writing, and when the Roman Catholic church took control of Europe, the Celtic territory of Lusitania was not spared.

Lusitanian was the Celtic language spoken by my father's ancestors.[6] When my father began classes in Gaelic, he found

---

[6]Though there is some controversy about whether Lusitanian was a Celtic language, after long study we are convinced of the case that it is. Key references here are the research of professor Dan Bradley, principal investig-

a remarkable connection between its vocabulary and some Portuguese vernacular words. The Celts spoke their own language until the Roman occupation, and the shift away from it happened when the Romans became Catholic.

The divine innocence of the Celtic bards was then replaced by the belligerence and disgust of the Catholic priests. Celtic poetry was replaced by the Latin Mass, attendance at which was compulsory according to the commandments of the new Latin clergy. The beautiful poetry of the Celtic Lusitanians gave way to insulting language with an abysmal ignorance of the sense of poetry. The Lusitanians had to renounce their own doctrines in favour of distorted facts. Beautiful, emotional words became objects of disgust by being associated with obscenity.

Because there is no information on the subject, it took my father a lifetime, and then lessons in Gaelic, to finally understand that the allegedly obscene words in Portuguese vocabulary in fact communicate the poetic feelings of the ancient Lusitanos. For instance, the poetic Celtic or Lusitanian Conna—the name of the goddess of fertility—became an obscene word for vagina. Similarly, Celts loved to make love under the sacred oak, which in Portuguese is *carvalho*. As a result, *caralho* is the

---

ator of the Institute of Genetics at Trinity College, Dublin, whose theory is that the Celts arrived from the Iberian Peninsula at the end of the Ice Age; Bryan Sykes' book *Blood of the Isles* (2006); and the work of professor Stephen Oppenheimer, a British paediatrician, geneticist, and writer.

In addition, based on anthropological studies of the mythology of the ancient Celts, my father and I have also managed to connect the Celtic mythology of the Irish stories—including the festival of the three *F*s—to origins in what today is Portugal, which adds further weight to the case that Lusitanian was, in fact, a Celtic language.

vernacular word for penis.

In English we see the same metamorphosis. According to Geraldine Taylor-Wood of *ShiningBRIGHT* magazine, the spring is the source of the sacred river Kennett (derived from the ancient word *cunte*), which was the source of all life. Swallowhead Spring, at the river's source, has a regular cycle of ebb and flow, always running dry in winter, and represented the vagina of the goddess.

Fortunately, the habit of the Catholic Church to degrade Celtic traditions did not take root in the north of Portugal. There, the vernacular of the northern people, *nortenhos*, shows their Lusitanian roots and is a form of patriotism. Their frank speaking of Portuguese rude words shows that they are still deeply connected to their Celtic dialect and mythology. Another remarkable coincidence that shows the Celtic connection is that people in the north of Portugal don't pronounce the letter *V*. My great-grandmother, who was from the north, never called my father *Ivo*, but always *Ibo*, just as the northerners never say *vaca* (cow), but always *baca*. *Vinho* (wine) becomes *binho*, and so on. This is an inheritance from the Celtic language.

13. The Celts: The alienated culture

The Celts dominated Europe during the Bronze Age and introduced the Europeans to the art and techniques of steelworking. They had the most famous philosophers of antiquity, the druids, and their society was the most advanced, when we consider that the most sublime achievement of any civilisation is for men to be born free.

Greeks and Romans

The religious ceremonies of the Celts took place in open spaces, close to sacred sights in the natural landscape, such as oak trees and springs. A remarkable contrast with the supposedly advanced cultures of their contemporaries was that Celts did not have a slave class. A warrior could become a slave if his enemies captured him, but every man was born free. Today, even in Australia, because of the Celtic influence we still find many surnames like "Freeman."

Celts also introduced wheeled vehicles to the ancient world. They brought novelty to the wheel by adding a steel rim to support it and give it durability and strength, and from there dramatically improved transportation in the ancient world with their four-wheeled wagons, which carried supplies and people.

The Celts' chariots of war had a distance of 4ft 8½in between them. Curiously, these are the standard truck dimensions on North American railroads. In fact, the Celts who migrated from Ireland and Scotland to America, Australia, and New Zealand still used four-wheeled wagons. The two-wheeled chariot developed into the two-wheeled carts used today in harness racing (aka "the trots"), which still attracts crowds, especially among the Celtic population in Australia.

Celts were health-conscious

If you think diet, exercise, and hygiene are purely modern concerns, think again. The Greek historian Strabo explains that in Celtic society, "To be fat was socially unacceptable."

A distinguished Greek geographer, Strabo was born in Cappadocia in about 19 AD, and travelled through Europe, Egypt, and Asia. His great geographical work of seventeen books contains a full account of the manners and governments of many different people of the time. His material came from his own observations and enquiries, as well as from the geographic works of Hecateus, Artemidorus, Endoxius and Eratosthenes, all of which are now lost, and from the writings of historians and poets. Strabo's work remains invaluable to us today.

According to Strabo, if a Celtic warrior gained too much weight, he had to pay a fine to his tribe. Celts were also promoters of personal hygiene and the inventors of soap. They invented a rotary mill to grind flour for bread, and pioneered the preservation of food with salt. Salzburg, Austria, was the castle of salt, and smoked ham was one of its specialties.

The Celtic armies defeated the Romans and sacked the city

of Rome in about 390 BC. Then, according to Pausanias, they seized the sanctuary of Apollo in 279 BC. They plundered the shrine at Delphi, melting down gold and silver, and kept an army on the proceeds. Once, a mercenary army of Gauls fighting for Alexander the Great was asked, by the great general, if they were afraid of anything, and their answer was, "We are only afraid that the sky might fall on us." This response reflects the true spirit of a Celtic warrior who had been trained from an early age not to be afraid of death. Any warrior confronted with the option of a long life followed by death in obscurity would instead choose a short life continued in immortality through the *fados*, in which the bards would sing of their accomplishments in war. The Celtic dream was to die in wartime during battle, surrounded by comrades and poets, leaving behind a hundred dead enemies on the battlefield.

The supremacy of Celtic poetry is still tested today in the annual European festival of the Eurovision Song Contest, which Ireland, the world's only independent Celtic country, has dominated for more than twenty years.

The Celts were wonderful people

It is always difficult to write about a culture that decided never to commit its knowledge to writing. How can we say the Celts were wonderful people, the reader may ask, when they left no records of their early history by which we might know it? But the Celts still exist today, and they are indeed wonderful people.

The contemporary Celts have inherited from their ancestors a deep feeling for poetry. Hitherto, poets had been the only instructors of the Celtic world, and this continued when the trajectory of that world changed radically with the Roman invasion. In all Celtic nations, heroic poetry flourished, as did the spirit of heroism. The heroes were followed by the bards, who sung of their deeds and gave birth to epics. Along with the hymns by which they celebrated their gods at festivals, the Celtic tribes also gave birth to the heroic ode.

Fado: The songs of long ago

The Celts were one of the world's most imaginative people, when it came to poetry. They listened to the *fados* of their bards with joy, and thought of the time when their own achievements might entitle them to similar honours.

Today, the *fado* still conveys strong feelings, not only to the Portuguese but also to the tourists in Lisbon who visit the *casas tipicas de fados* (typical *fado* houses) where the Portuguese storytellers travel back in time to the wonderful Celtic world of the Lusitanos. In these mystic houses, one can listen to the ancient melodies with the accompaniment of the classic guitar and also the Portuguese guitar, which is an evolution of the harp, and have a romantic candlelight dinner of Celtic food.

Such a meal will include garlic sausage (*murcela*, from the Gaelic *mucus*, a sacred pig), cooked on a plate over a naked flame, and sangria, the favourite drink of the pagan gods. Lusitanian sangria is a sweet juice that was the fabled drink of ancient sacrifices that conferred immortality on those who partook in it, and consists of wine mixed with lemonade and slices of orange. This mixture represents the drink of the ritual sacrifices: blood mixed with honey and slices of Hesperidium.[1] The word *sangria* comes from *sangrar* (to bleed), and men who were allowed to drink it received an increase of beauty, strength, and swiftness, becoming in some measure godlike.

The Olympic fado

When religion breathed into a sublime song, the air of Paradise became the fado.

Fado is a Celtic word, and as with the Celtic people, its story has been lost in the obscurity of prehistory.

We know from the Greeks that *fado* were performed at the ritual of Dionysus, the orgy. Folk dramas were all based on a sequence of three stages. First was a deadly battle between two warriors, where one is killed but then restored to life. This story and its associated rituals derived from the belief that an aged king must be slain to give new life to the soil. Kings were put to death after their term of rulership. "*Rei morto, rei posto,*" is a Portuguese saying still used today, meaning that the death of a new king brings his replacement with a new king.

At Mount Olympus, Dionysus is the *lusios*—the liberator. He is the god of wine, but also of fertility, and gives the assurance that death is not the end of all. He embodies life that is stronger than death, and became the centre of belief in immortality. As the liberator, he represents the power of natural fertility. In the Baal cult of the Celtic Beltane festival, he rep-

---

[1] The order *Hesperidiae* was an order of plants to which belonged the citrus fruits, including the orange.

169

resents the god who died and rose again.

Life and death, light and darkness, summer and winter, and old king and young king are all pairs that represent the play between decline and renewal that is at the centre of the rituals of Dionysus where the *fado* were performed. The rituals were of unrestrained merrymaking and revelry: they involved excessive drinking, singing, dancing, the meat of sacrificed animals, and sexual promiscuity. Later folk dramas associated with these festivals included satire and were filled with crude practical jokes and ready banter between the actors.

These rituals were definitely popular, since they were extended throughout Europe, but because of the disturbances created by large numbers of worshippers, during the Roman occupation, the Senate forbade them. Nevertheless, such revelry still exists today: the concept of the orgy or bacchanal will last forever. We no longer sacrifice the king, but in some countries we still sacrifice the bull in the bullfight. The dances of the Dionysian rituals still exist in many countries, especially in the mountains of Europe, and the sorrow (the lamentation of villagers at the king's death) survives mainly in Portugal as its national song, the *fado*, which persists almost in its original form.

Fado: Ancient songs of the story of life

The *fado* sings of the tragedy of cyclical life. Long ago, the Celts conceived this most comprehensive form of music to describe the three stages of life. We are born, we live, and we die. For birth we sing the happy *fado*, during life we speak the *fado*, and after life we mourn though *fado*.

The most popular form of the *fado* today is its serious expression, which gives us the sorrow of tragedy. The other forms are the *fado falado*, which is spoken, and the humorous *fado comico*. Modern research says laughter is a natural healer, and the tradition of the *fado comico* shows that my father's ancestors already knew this thousands of years ago.

The *fado* can be performed by one or more *fadistas* (*fado* singers and, as in ancient times, the crude jokes and ready responses between actors and comedians are still part of what we today call *desgarradas*, as in *o fado a desgarrada* (a battle of words between two singers, much like a modern-day rap battle). Even today, *fado* is still very dramatic.

Dionysus was the patron of drama. So who were the originators of *fado*—the Greeks or the Celts? The answer is neither, since the origins of the *fado* and its associated rituals are lost in the obscurity of the Neolithic period. European civilisation was not created in just a few centuries: its roots are deeper by thousands of years.

Archaeologists tell us that there is evidence of phallic obsessions represented in artefacts and representations back to the Neolithic period. The Celts obviously knew of this long heritage, since the songs they called *fado* used to be connected with promiscuity. In Irish Gaelic, *fado* means "long ago." Could this refer to the songs of Celtica Atlanta, the lost paradise of Plato?

Today, the Irish still have *fado*, but it was in Portugal that these songs regained their golden age. The Portuguese *fado* is famous all over the world, and even in Japan it has found a large following. The dance of the antique Irish rituals, though, the river dance, remains very strong, and the Lord of the Dance has become the most famous dance spectacle to tour the world.

In Portugal, dance still remains in its primitive, folkloric stage—the fandango represents the contest of two men over a woman, where the woman is a symbol for the motherland. And we know that the *faena*—the bullfights—are still a strong tradition in Iberia. So Portugal's Lusitanians still maintain the festival of the three *F*s: *fado*, *fandango*, and *faena*, which corresponds with the triple sacrifice of the *suovetaurilia* (see p.32). Yet, many Portuguese academics still do not know the story of their national song, saying that *fado* originated in Lisbon and is only four hundred years old. Others even say it came from Brazil only 150 years ago.

The religion of the Celts

The Celts were inclined to festivity, even in religion, and served the gods less in spirit than in outward ceremonies. Their religion had little influence on their morals and in governing their thoughts—all it required was a belief in the gods and in a future existence, abstention from gross crimes, and observance of prescribed rites.

The simplicity of Celtic manners, and some obscure notions they had of a supreme god who hated and punished evil but loved and rewarded good, at first served to maintain good morals and piety. Such ideas were later exalted and systematised in poetry and philosophy, and improvement then spread from the cultivated classes through the mass of the people.

In the most enlightened period of Celtic society, clear ideas of the unity, omniscience and omnipresence, holiness, goodness, and justice of the deity prevailed. So did the sense that it was necessary to worship him through virtue and purity of heart. The moral system of some individuals among the Celts was equally pure. Their moral precepts were at first expressed in sententious maxims such as, "Die standing like a man," a phrase still popular in Portugal. The statue *The Dying Cuchulain* in the General Post Office in Dublin shows the famous Celtic warrior bound to a stone so he could die standing, exemplifying his faith in his religion and also his bravery. The word *faia* is a Portuguese word synonymous with courage, and from the eighteenth century it developed into *fadista*—the fado singer.

Love of freedom

The Celts' love of freedom sprang from their good fortune in having lived so long without being oppressed or in fear of other nations, as well as from their natural vivacity of spirit. It was this spirit that made their small armies invincible against the powerful and organised Roman legions and caused Viriato to refuse a crown when the Romans recognised him as king of the Lusitanos. Celtic freedom was the work of nature and the consequence of their originally matriarchal mode of living.

The Celts' first chieftains were considered fathers of families, to whom obedience was willingly paid in return for protection and favours. Assemblies of the people decided important affairs. Each man was a master in his own house, and in early times no taxes were paid, but as the chieftains strove continually to extend their powers, individuals were ultimately compelled to relinquish their authority to the powerful chieftains that arose, and government inclined more or less to aristocracy. Citizens were attached to their tribe, which was governed by wise laws rather than arbitrary power.

Some individual Celts were known for their moral purity. For instance, on the day of his wedding, Viriato, leader of the Lusitanos, took his wife and left the superb banquet his rich father-in-law had prepared for the occasion, because he realised some of the guests were Romans. As a warrior, he disbelieved in doing business with the enemy and having them at his party: their attendance seemed the height of insolence. After this diplomatic incident, Viriato's father-in-law, Astopas, reconsidered his stance and put himself and his private army at the service of the Lusitanian cause under Viriato's leadership.

Ninety years later it was a similarly noble love for his free country that prompted Vercingetorix to tell Julius Caesar that he would rather die than hold a despotic sway over Gaul. This nobility also inspired Ambiorix to choose to serve the tribes and the Celtic laws rather than his own interests.

My great-grandmother, the prophetess

A prophet is a person inspired or instructed by God to announce future events. Sceptics disbelieve that some people can make declarations of events to come. But when my father was born, my grandfather's mother delivered a prediction with a loud voice, in a four-line stanza:

Ivo tem que se chamar	Ivo must be called
o meu neto illuminado	my grandson, enlightened
Por sete luzes sagradas	by seven sacred lights
Para contar historia do Fado	to tell the *fado*'s history

Seven is a mystical number, and Portugal a living museum. My father was the seventh grandchild of my great-grandmother when he was born in 1947 in Lisbon, which was then the capital of a European imperial power. At that time, Portugal was one of the richest countries in Europe. The colonial empire, along with Portugal's neutrality during the Second World War, had seen the safes of its government and private banks crammed with gold bars. Some of this, too, was the result of golden deals the Portuguese fascists had done with the Nazis.

After the catastrophe of the war, in which millions of people died fighting for liberty, in Portugal the Catholic Church protected the dictatorship and the kingdom of half a dozen rich families prevailed. Despite all the country's accumulated wealth, Salazar and his regime failed to provide the people with necessities such as electricity. In 1947, men already knew of atomic energy, but my father was born in a house without electricity. That house had been built in 1757, and belonged to my grandmother's mother, who was a weaver.

Three women organised seven naked flames by which my grandmother would give birth. This did not happen by chance: it was God's wish and the beginning of my father's *fado*. Fire, according to the Bible, is God's presence, and the three women, in conformity with Celtic mythology, represented the three goddesses who are supposed to preside over the birth and life of men.

Portugal is indeed a place of mysticism. We find there seven rivers, seven windmills, and even the old tradition of the seven skirts, which the women still wear in the beautiful seaside town of Nazaré. This practice is related to the ancient Sumerian myth of Inanna, goddess of love, fertility, and warfare. There is also the ritual of the seven gates, which is related to the queen of heaven and earth, where at each gate the goddess removes a piece of clothing.

Portugal is today a living museum because of its continued use of these mythological traditions relating to events that occurred more than five thousand years ago.

The Celtic Olympic Games: Myth or reality?

Because history always repeats itself, this message is directed to those who trace their ancestry from Ireland, Great Britain, and places from Portugal to Poland. My father tells me that we must remember the common market that came before Greece and the Roman invasion of Europe, which was the ancient Celtic European civilisation. Even the Mycenaeans, the heroes of Homer, and the Romans themselves shared some of the mythology of the great Indo-European family.

Some readers may think that my father's fervour to pass down his Celtic culture has led him to invent a hypothetical Celtic Olympics. Yet, there is indeed historical evidence that the Celtic people had their counterpart to the Ancient Olympic Games.

As I explained before, the Ancient Olympics developed from funeral games—the same origin as the Lughnasadh games that resembled them. In Irish Gaelic, *cluiche* means *games* and *cáinteach* means *funeral.* The Celts, like the Mycenaean Greeks, believed in life after death, and a place of peace and harmony— the Elysian land. Along with the scribes of the Avesta, they also called the other world a place of truth.

I find a remarkable similarity between these ancient beliefs and my father's education. My grandfather, a Lusitano, used to say, "*um dia, la iremos para a terra da verdade*" ("One day, we will go to the land of the truth"). This contrasts with the infernal and purgatorial places that my father describes his school as, and about which he had to learn. According to the Catholic Church, hell is the lower region for the dead, and purgatory a place where souls are purified of their venal sins.

The Celtic way of thinking is also related to the cycle of life, death, and rebirth, which is the reason "two never happens without three". This philosophy is related to the idea of fertility. Cluich Cáinteach, Lughnasadh, and the Olympics were games that promoted fertility.

Could we really believe that the Celts shared these beliefs with the Greeks, but that only the Greeks had the capacity to organise sporting events? History misrepresents the Celts. At home, I have a book, *The Olympic Spirit*,[2] written by Greek author Elsi Spathari, which says that in Egypt organised games were unknown in historical times. Spathari's source is the testimony of Herodotus, the father of history, who visited Egypt in the sixth century BC. It is because of this that the evolution of simple exercises into organised games focused on an ideal is regarded as a purely Greek achievement.

These Greek academics show poor knowledge of other cultures of the time, and also the meaning of the games. They ignore the fact that religious sporting festivals were also found in other pagan cultures. The Celts, for instance, believed that the gods moved with a divine ease that cost the body no exertion, but that men's actions demanded muscular effort and were accomplished only with labour and difficulty. This way of thinking led to their development as a race of great athletes

---

[2]Elsi Spathari, *The Olympic Spirit* (Athens: Adam Editions, 1992).

with a fanatical attitude to weight control.

The Celts also had more sporting events than the Greeks. In fact, some of the modern Olympic events, which had never been part of the Ancient Olympics, were already familiar to the Celts. Take pole vaulting for an example: according to Celtic mythology, Oengus, the god of love, gave to the *fianna* warrior Diarmaid a magical spear with which he could vault over warriors who were chasing him, and an enchanted cloak so that his girlfriend could travel undetected. So we can see that, thousands of years ago, the Celts already knew the technique of pole vaulting, which was never included in the ancient games of the Greeks.

Hammer-throwing, another modern Olympic event, was also popular among the Celtic tribes. Cú Chulainn is said to have taken hold of a chariot wheel by the axle, revolved it rapidly around his head, and then thrown it further than any other athlete. Later, wheel throwing was replaced with the sport of hurling a boulder, a water-worn, roundish stone of considerable size, attached to the end of a wooden handle. Then there is the triple jump, which we can see is linked to Celtic belief through the adage that "two never happens without three."

So, the Celts had the same mythology, and more sporting events. How about the Greeks' reverence for the time of the games? As we know, the Greeks had the *Hieromenia*, the sacred truce, which obliged all wars to cease so the games could take place. The Celts had a similar tradition: we know that in Ireland, if a man disturbed the Lughnasadh games, he was sentenced to death and not even the king could save his life. In Greece, too, the Olympic rituals dictated that those who violated the peace should be punished. Peace-breakers not only disturbed public harmony, but also damaged the accord between gods and men.

In fact, the reason behind the sporting ritual was to assuage the gods' anger and secure the continuation of fertility. We must remember that, according to pagan belief as well as the Old Testament, the deluge had taken place to punish mankind for its iniquity. Before the Sydney Olympics in 2000, Australians recalled this ancient event and sent one of their athletes to the United Nations, calling for a worldwide truce during the games.

14. The remembrance of Lughnasadh in Portugal

A feira da luz—The fair of light

In contrast to the Olympics, which disappeared for 1,700 years, the Celtic festival of Lughnasadh has never ceased to exist. It has suffered some changes over the centuries, but still takes place throughout Europe, especially in Portugal.

A festa da Senhora da Luz—The festival of Our Lady of Light

Lughnasadh is named after Lugh, who decreed that funeral games be held in honour of his foster mother. For most Celtic scholars, Lugh is the sun god who presides over the sciences and the arts. Julius Caesar called him Mercury-Hermes. Some authors have claimed that Lugh is not the sun god, because in Celtic mythology the sun is feminine.

Because our Celtic ancestors left little in the way of writing, it is difficult to reconstruct our history with maximum acuity. Nevertheless, despite the substitution of Gaelic with Latin, Celtic scholars can still reconstruct some historical events. We know that when Catholics changed the gods into saints, Lugh became connected with Saint Anthony. But the sun god still keeps a female name because, in the place of the sun god, we have Our Lady of the Light.

At the same time, the sports stadium *Lisboa e Benfica*, one of the most famous football stadiums in Europe, is called by Benfica acolytes the Cathedral of Light. This was where my father started his semi-professional soccer career in the *juvenal* division, at the same time the Benfica seniors were one of the best teams in the world. In Portugal, there is no historical information available on the mythology of my father's ancestors, so he had no idea that this sacred place of the modern football religion had also been the holy fields of his ancestors, thousands of years ago. Obviously, the stadium got its name, *O estadio da luz* (The Stadium of Light) from the suburb where it is situated, Luz. But *luz* also means light, and not far from the stadium, every year, the Portuguese celebrate the festival of Our Lady of the Light—who today is identified with Mary, the mother of Jesus.

Celtic culture in Australia

Australia is losing the memory of its Celtic heritage. Although most Australians are of Celtic ancestry, schools in Australia still ignore the Celtic influence. How is it possible for such a great culture to be forgotten? It could be due to the negligence of the country's leaders, a lack of attention on the part of academics, and the pressure of media magnates to turn a great nation into a "great *alienation*".[1]

At the beginning of the twentieth century, the Celtic language, predominantly Irish Gaelic, was widely understood in Australia, especially in Victoria. Celts love style, and their reverence for eloquence is unlimited, according to numerous books that can be found in the State Library of Victoria. But in the twenty-first century, Australian leaders give Celts the impression that they despise the culture. Regardless of the vast knowledge accumulated over the years, and Australians' natural capacity for learning, Australians don't learn a word about the great people who were responsible for building and providing a foundation for this modern country.

The sun: A vital radiation

Solar radiation furnishes the earth with heat and light, causing animals and plants to grow, evaporating the oceans and rivers to create clouds and rain, and playing an important role in the production of winds and many other phenomena that are vital to the existence of life. Scientists have discovered that what keeps the sun producing its seemingly infinite energy is its natural atomic reactor. They have also calculated that it can maintain its present rate of output for more than 10 billion years.

---

[1] "Alienation, defined as a rejection of social institutions and processes, plays an important role in sociological theory and research. Here a measure of the degree of alienation is examined with respect to mass media exposure, interest in sensational content, and gratifications obtained from the media." Jack McLeod, Scott Ward, and Karen Tancill, "Alienation and Uses of the Mass Media," *The Public Opinion Quarterly* 29, no. 4 (Winter 1965–1966), 583.

So, modern men don't need to be afraid that the sun will disappear. In fact, the main thing we have to be concerned about is not to expose our skin excessively to solar radiation, to avoid burns and even skin cancer.

Obviously, the Celts didn't have today's scientific knowledge, but they understood very well that the sun is vital to the wealth of the world. So, it is understandable that they considered the sun a god, adoring it with profound reverence. In fact, every nation in antiquity engaged in this kind of heliolatry.

The Lusitanians were the warriors of the sun. Translated from the old Celtiberian dialect, the word Lusitania combines the names of two solar deities, Lugh and Áine, the goddess of summer. Like many other lost civilisations, they portrayed the circle of life with reference to three positions of the sun's daily movement, sunrise, noon, and sunset.

The swastika: An ancient solar emblem

A few ancient nations across the globe created the swastika to represent the three daily solar positions, representing the circle of life: creation, death, and rebirth. Thousands of years ago, people across the globe, from Japan to America and Europe, all venerated this symbol. The Celts also adopted a tradition of saluting the sun with their right arm. On the Iberian Peninsula, archaeologists have discovered carved stones showing warriors with their right arms raised straight in the direction of the rising sun. In fact, what the Nazis copied with their salute was the ancient European warriors' practice of saluting their beloved sun god.

Every fascist movement in Europe recreated this ancient custom: Mussolini in Italy, Franco in Spain, and Salazar in Portugal. When my father was a student in Portugal, during the weekends at the *Mocidade Portuguesa* (Portuguese Youth—a kind of government Boy Scout organisation) they had a similar greeting: "*O sol invicto*" ("The unconquered sun").

Appearing new and vigorous every day in the east, ascending into the sky dressed in red and driving his golden chariot, pulled by two flaming horses, and reaching maturity at the vertical point of heavens (the zenith), the sun drives on to a bygone age, gradually declining into the darkness of the deadly night in the west, only to be reborn at daybreak.

The corn god is related to the sun. During summer, after the reaping of corn, he sinks into the otherworld's deadly abyss (winter) and swims back from it to the east where he is reborn in spring. This mythology also relates to Jesus Christ, whose story of resurrection is based on ancient traditions of sun worship.

Indo-Europeans worshipped Dyas or Dyaus, the sun god, who they portrayed as a warrior dressed in golden or red armour. *Deus* is the Portuguese word for God, *dia* is the Irish Gaelic equivalent. *Dias* is also the Portuguese word for days, because day is light—the god's presence.

Faena

Even Zeus, the father of the Greek gods, transformed himself into a bull to seduce Europa. The Celtiberian bullfight is a survival of the Celtic ritual of fertility. The Celts formalised the rules, which are still maintained today, that apply to anyone who is prepared to become a matador—a bullfighter. These rules were designed to subject the fighter to arduous labour and pain, in the belief that the harder the performance of their sacrifice, the more divine protection they would receive.

Ancestors of the faena (bullfight)

Fion Fair, brilliant. Anyone who looks at him must have his eyes closed tight.

Fianna Killer of monsters. Magician and poet.

Fion Chief of the Fianna.

Lugh or Lugo Ancient hero and High King of Ireland. The "long arm" of the sun god.

Celtic mythology allows us to understand the meaning of the *faena* ritual. To accomplish the difficult task of the ritual of sacrificing the bull, the services were employed of the best warriors, the Fianna, or in Lusitano, the *Faia*. Today, the matador and his *quadrilha* gang (*peoes de brega* or briga represent the ancient warriors. Nowadays, the matador and his group are still brave men, equal in courage to any warriors of the past.

Bullfighting is a ritual, not a sport

The Iberian bullfight is known as the *festa brava*. No enthusiast of bullfighting in Portugal or Spain considers it a sport, as it was and continues to be a ritual.

All famous civilisations of the past have worshipped bulls. For them, the bull was connected with the sun and with fertility. Primitive men would be excited with fear on approaching a bull. The horns were considered a symbol of fertility, and men related to bulls, believing they possessed the three fundamental qualities required of a sacrifice—huge size, courage, and fertility.

In many civilisations, the bull god was offered as a sacrifice to the sun god, with the aim of producing abundant crops. The blood of the sacred bull fell on the earth, producing barley bread and barley ale. The Catholic Church still performs a ritual venerating the corn god in the form of the Eucharist, consecrating bread in the sacrifice of the Mass.

Ancient kings and warriors wore bull horns into battle as a symbol of power and fertility, and the epithet *El* in *El tauro* is an adjective expressing the quality ascribed to the bull, and is placed before *Don* as a reinforcement of that power. The name *El*, implying a quality attached to a bull, was used by the last Portuguese king together with *Don*, which is a title in the Iberian Peninsula formerly given to noblemen only but now used much more widely. It comes from *dominium, dominion,* or *domain,* which references sovereign or supreme authority, and the power of governing or controlling. *El Rei Don Afonso Henriques* was the first Portuguese king. *El Rei Don Carlos* was the king assassinated by the republicans.

The matador

In the imagination of the Celtic bards, the bullfighter represented the sun. This is why, even today, the matador must dress in an expensive and sumptuous outfit of golden embroidery. He represents Lugh, the sun god of the long arm (the sword or spear) and, according to the sacred rules, he must kill the black bull, representing bad weather, so the sacred blood will impregnate the motherland and produce good crops.

As we can see, the *faena* symbolises the victory of the sun over bad weather, and the continuation of fertility. Many people still believe red is the colour the bull prefers to attack. But since veterinarians found out bulls are colour-blind, we must look to Celtic mythology once more for the reason that the red cape is used. Red represents the sun god—the sunrise. The Japanese have the same idea, as we can see by looking at the Japanese flag, which belongs to the "land of the rising sun." For the Celts, red was also the colour of death and war. The red cape is the instrument the matador uses to challenge the bull until the final, deadly strike.

Today, the Spanish and the Portuguese are the people who strictly maintain the Celtic ritual of the *faena*. Many condemn the Iberians for this ritual but, contrary to common belief, the bullring is a place where the bull dies with dignity.

The bullring is not an abbatoir, which is a slaughterhouse where a butcher is employed to kill animals for meat. While in the abbatoir, a bull is tied to a pole preceding its death: in the bullring, the matador is not allowed to strike the bull unless the animal is attacking. He is not allowed to stick his sword in the bull unless he is in danger. In fact, to strike a bull in motion is very dangerous, and many matadors have died or suffered serious injuries in the attempt. If the bull shows great courage, the public can also demand an *indulto*, or pardon, and in this case the bull will live to reproduce, because the sublime intention of the ritual is not merely to kill the bull, but to kill him according to the three sacred rules: generosity, frankness, and politeness. This has always been the nature of the sacrifice, and will be for generations to come.

Taking the bull by the horns: 5,000 years of history

The ritual of the bullfight, like the sacred wrestling ritual of the Ancient Olympics, can be traced back to the *Epic of Gilgamesh*, where Enkidu sprang and seized the bull of heaven by its horns. Then, seizing the bull by the thick of its tail, Gilgamesh thrust his dagger into its neck and between its horns.

Like the Cretans, the Celts considered the bull's horns to be the fulcrum of fertility, where the animal's magic was concentrated. *O pegador* (chief of the *forcados*), the bull catcher, receives the full force of the bull's impact—many bulls weigh around 650kg—and keeps holding the horns, absorbing the power and the virility of the animal for his benefit and the benefit of his group. Only in Portugal can the public observe this part of the ritual. But in Portugal, matadors are no longer allowed to kill bulls. For that, they must go across the border to neighbouring Spain.

The *forcado*, like the matador, is a man of fortitude. Each must possess the strength of mind that enables them to encounter danger with coolness and courage. The *forcado* must adopt a state of fearful excitement to face the bull's approach, and after successfully performing his heroic deed, he feels like a great achiever. Respected by men and adored by women, at that moment, the *forcado* is the symbol of power and fertility. After more than 5,000 years, little about this fertility ritual has changed.

Portugal: The territory of Lusitania

Portugal's location at the westernmost point of continental Europe—"where the land ends and the sea begins"—made it a gathering place for invaders who wanted to enter the continent by land, and its long coastline enticed seafarers to establish themselves there.

Greek geographers gave the name *Iberian* to tribes that live in the region; it is probably connected to that of the Ebro or Iberus river. Subsequently, these tribes gave their name to the entire peninsula. Its main countries are Spain and Portugal, the British territory of Gibraltar in the south, and Andorra in the eastern Pyrenees.

The prehistoric people of the region, the Ibero, were in direct contact with the important civilisations of antiquity, and couldn't help but be influenced by the diverse cultures and religious beliefs of those who came to trade with or to invade them. According to historians, some Gauls (a Celtic tribe) left Gaul (France) behind and settled in northern and central Spain between the ninth and sixth centuries BC. They established themselves in Portugal and Galicia, making these Celtic territories. And when the Romans started to invade the Lusitanian territory between the two main rivers, the Douro and the Tejo, they noticed that the Lusitanians were not a Celtiberian tribe but a genuine Celtic people. They mingled less with the locals, and managed to keep the Celtic culture intact.

Lusitanian chronology

Possibly around 1000 BC. Celts arrive in the Iberian peninsula. The exact date is lost in the obscurity of prehistory.

ca 900 BC. Phoenician and later Carthaginian domination of the coast.

650 BC. Greek Ionians arrived in Lisbon and started an emporium for trade.

139 BC–409 AD. Roman domination starts after the death of Viriato.

409 AD. Roman domination ends with the barbarian invasions of the Alans, Vandals, Sueves, and Visigoths.

711–1247 AD. Moorish occupation.

997 AD. Bermudo II, King of Léon, reconquers the territory between the Douro and Minho rivers in what is now northern Portugal.

1128–1185 AD. Rule of the House of Burgundy.

1139 AD. Don Afonso Henriques (1109–1185) is crowned the first king of Portugal.

Seven: A mystical Lusitanian number

In the year 1147, the ancient territory of the Lusitanians, which is situated between the Douro and Tagus (Tejo) rivers, and includes the cities of Santarem and Lisbon, was recovered from the Moors by conquest. This was seven centuries after the dismantling of the Roman province of Lusitania, which began around 409 AD. In the year 1247, Alfonso III finally recovered the territory of the ancient Roman Lusitanian frontiers, and finally all of Lusitania was again ruled by the Lusitanos.

In 1947, my father was born in Lisbon with the sacred mission of learning and teaching the Portuguese the sacred culture of the Celts. In Gaelic, his name, Ivo, signifies the bowman. The yew, an evergreen tree allied to the conifers and indigenous to Europe and Asia, was used for the bow. The tree yields a hard and durable timber also used for cabinetwork. In an allegorical sense, one called Ivo aims people towards a goal: he is the archer, who sends a missile towards an object.

Lusitania is a place of faith and adventure. The idea that the land incarnates a goddess is a universal notion, but it must have been particularly deeply rooted in the land of Lusitania, because even now the inhabitants still hold to it. The concept of spiritual regeneration is still implanted in the heart of the Portuguese: in no other Catholic country did the cult of the Virgin take root as it has in Portugal, home of the phenomenon of Our Lady of Fatima.

Apparitions

On 13 May 1917, *Nossa Senhra de Fatima* (Our Lady of Fatima) appeared to three *pastorinhos* (little shepherds). She was bright as the sun, and sparkling like spring water. Long, long ago, at Merceana (*merce* means *mercy*), according to legend, a shepherd had a vision in which a shepherd perceived the forms and the bright colour of Our Lady of Piety (*piedade*) around a bull that had fallen down on its knees. These Christian apparitions and the cults of Our Lady of the Rock (*Senhora da Rocha*) and Our Lord of the Rooster (*Senhor do Galo*), which harmonise with their surroundings of oaks, bulls, spring waters and so on, hark back to pagan times and demonstrated the survival of Celtic mythology.

According to history, long ago, before the Catholic Church was formed, the people of Lusitania already possessed intense qualities of devotion. Analysing their religious beliefs, we can see how today's Portuguese have received much from their Lusitano ancestors, who were Celts. And yet, less than 250 years ago, this book, *Chariot of Knowledge*, would have condemned me as the author to suffer at the stake, burned by the holy fire of the Catholic Inquisition. And before the revolution of 25 April 1974, I would have been violently forced behind the ramparts of a political jail.

The Church can burn books and academics can keep people in the dark; governments can prevent people from teaching others. But no one can interrupt cosmic communication or stop culture being transmitted through blood. This may be why, any time my father sings his Celtic *fados*, his people understand and say that he is singing like a true Lusitano.

Despite innumerable invasions by different tribes and beliefs, the Portuguese still have no doubt of their Lusitanian ancestry. Although they now speak a Latin language, they are still deeply rooted in their Celtic inheritance. Bearing witness to that heritage, last century, in the city of Viseu, a monument was erected to the hero Viriato, the Celtic demigod of the Lusitanian nation.

The Portuguese are not alone in worshipping Celtic leaders. Spain has also built a statue of Viriato. The French have a similar statue paying homage to Vercingetorix, the Celtic chieftain who fought Caesar. The Belgians erected a statue of Ambiorix, and Ireland has its statue of Cú Chulainn at the General Post Office in Dublin. Even England has a fine statue to a Celtic heroine, Boudica, giving reverence to that country's Celtic natives: the Britons were a Celtic tribe. These monuments prove to all of Europe that there is still a Celtic consciousness and awareness. But the Celtic realm is not exclusive to Europeans: it also spread to Australia and North America.

My father's good friend, the famous martial arts teacher Victor Jones (aka Bob Jones) a few years ago had a vision that appeared by divine agency, about Europe, the land of reverie, and awakened with a new interpretation of the word *Celt*:

Combine Europe's Lost Tribes

The origins of names

Paris: The city of light

One example of how Celtic history has fallen into obscurity is in the oft-forgotten story of the founding of Paris, today arguably the greatest city of Europe and certainly one of the world's most magnificent. The city's origins are immersed in obscurity, but most credit is given to the account that a wandering Celtic tribe settled on the banks of the Seine around the fifth century BC. They built huts on the island of the city, to which they retired with their flocks and herds when the neighbouring tribes made incursions upon them. F some reason not clearly explained, they took the name *Parisii*. When Julius Caesar conquered Gaul in 52 BC, he found a tribe of Parisii with a capital of Lutetium (Lutetia), connected to the shores by two bridges. They defended themselves bravely against the Romans, but were overcome by the legions' superior numbers.

Caesar rebuilt the town, which had been nearly destroyed when the Parisii burned their huts and abandoned the city. The Romans surrounded it with walls and further defended it by erecting two forts at the extremity of the bridges. The Gaelic deities were exchanged for Roman ones.

Civilisation in what is now Paris made rapid progress, and over the course of five hundred years of Roman domination, Lutetia rose to become a place of considerable importance, which was the capital of New Gaul. The Romans gave this stronghold the name *Lutetium*, which is a corruption of Lugdunum (the castle of Lugh). Lugh, again, is the god of sun and war according to Celtic mythology.

So, contrary to the popular assumption, it was not the Romans who founded Paris, but the Celts. Its name comes from the Parisi, a Celtic tribe. In the near future, my father intends to visit Paris and hopes the French media will open a debate about the city's Celtic heritage.

As a Celtic bard, my father will continue to sing his Celtic *fados*. The French love *fado* in Portuguese. Even if they may not understand the Portuguese language, in their subconscious they can go back to their Celtic roots, so they love *fado.*

The name "Portugal"

Um Pais a beira mar plantado (A country planted on the shoreline)

The former name of Portugal was Lusitania, and this is why the Portuguese still call themselves Lusitanos. The Lusitanians were a powerful Celtic tribe that opposed Roman occupation and interference. Never in the history of the Roman legions had they lost so many men against a small army as they did when fighting the Lusitanians. According to Irish history, the legendary Lusitanian leader Viriato defeated five entire Roman legions, a total of 25,000 men, with a force of just 6,000 warriors.

The name *Portugal* comes from two words: *Portus,* the name of the god of the sea, and *gal,* from *galos* (rooster). The rooster is the symbol of Portugal, and the rooster of Barcelos, a northern Portuguese city near Galicia, is the same as the *coq sportif,* the rooster of France.

It is said that one Celtic tribe left Gaul (France) and settled in Portugal and Galicia, which is now a province of Spain. The Romans gave the Gauls their name, which is connected to the same root as the Portuguese *galos,* because of their appreciation for the rooster. In fact, the rooster was sacred to the Celts, who believed that as it was the herald of the dawn, the cock was connected with the sun god. Country people also say that the cock crows three times before the death of a person, and the cock is also an excellent combatant and a symbol of virility. So the ancients held the rooster sacred.

Baron Pierre de Coubertin: Erudite or ignorant?

Baron Pierre de Coubertin, founder of the modern Olympics, is widely accepted as a great thinker. But what was behind the revival of the Olympic movement? Was it knowledge of history, or could it have been ignorance? We must look at both sides of the story, which includes examining not just the Greek origins of the games, but also their Celtic counterparts.

The Celtic influence on the Olympics is currently a subject that few are sympathetic to, particularly academics in Portugal and the rest of Europe. Only in Great Britain do we find those willing to examine it.

What is behind the tendency of these academics to disregard the story of their own heritage? One answer may be found in the holy ignorance involved in the catastrophe of the Inquisition.

The Inquisition

The Inquisition was a fanatical Catholic religious tribunal, ruled by psychopaths, thieves, and murderers, who burned people alive between the thirteenth and nineteenth centuries, and simultaneously obstructed the human intellect. It did this with the blessing of several popes, and had as its principal objective the confiscation of people's property for its own gain.

197

The Inquisition was a religious court of law. Called the Holy Inquisition or Holy Office *Sanctum Officium*, it was under the immediate direction of the papal chair. Its mission was supposedly to seek out heretics and adherents of false doctrines, and it pronounced dreadful sentences against these heretics' fortune, honour, and lives. There was no appeal.

The process of this tribunal differed entirely from that of civil courts. Informers were not only concealed, but were rewarded by the Inquisition, while the accused was obliged to be his own accuser. Suspected people were secretly seized and thrown into prison.

No better source of inquisitors could be found than the mendicant orders of monks, particularly the Franciscans and Dominicans. The Pope employed these monks to destroy the heretics and inquire into the conduct of bishops. Pope Gregory IX completed the design of his predecessors in 1233, and the Inquisition was successively introduced into several parts of Italy, some French provinces, and Spain and Portugal.

The Inquisitions of Spain and Portugal were the most remarkable of all those ferocious religious courts of the Middle Ages, and differed greatly from the others in their objects and organisation. The tribunals were admitted into Spain in the middle of the thirteenth century, but firm opposition to them, especially in Castille and Léon, caused the bishops to retain their exclusive jurisdiction on spiritual matters there.

There were three religious parties in Spain—Christians, Jews, and Muslims. Though the Moors still maintained possession of the last remnant of their empire—the kingdom of Granada—it was already threatened by Ferdinand and Isabelle. The Jews had their synagogues and, forming a distinct class in the principal cities of Spain, they dominated commerce. Jews were the lessees of the king and nobles, and suffered no oppression: they were subject only to a moderate capital tax, which they had been obliged to pay to the clergy since 1302.

The riches that the Jews had amassed by their industry caused great envy and hatred, which was nourished by the Catholic priests. The sermons of one fanatical monk, Fernand Martinez Nunz, who preached that the persecution of the Jews was a good work, were the principal cause of the popular tumults in many cities, and in 1391 and 1392, many Jews were robbed and murdered. Many submitted to baptism to save their lives. These Jews were the first victims of inquisitorial zeal. People long dead were condemned, and their children dishonoured and rendered incapable of holding any office, though they retained their property.

The inquisitorial council assembled every day, except on holidays, in the royal palace. Some officers, the *calificadores*, had the duty of explaining whether any act or opinion considered was contrary to Church doctrine. Others were lawyers who served a deliberative function. Inquisition sentences were definitive.

It was the duty of the *fiscal* (the equivalent of the modern-day district attorney—an inquisitor) to examine the witnesses, and to give information about criminals, demand their apprehension, and accuse them when seized. He was present at the examination of witnesses during torture, and at the meeting of judges where votes were taken.

Officials were sent by the court to arrest those accused. A *sequestrador*, who was obliged to give sureties to the office, kept an account of confiscated property. The receiver took money that came from the sale of sequestrated property and paid salaries and drafts on the Inquisition treasury. It has been calculated that in Spain at one stage there were more than twenty thousand officers of the Inquisition, called *familiars*, who served as spies and informers. From the moment that a prisoner was in the power of the Inquisition's court, he was cut off from the world. The prisons were called "holy houses" (*casas santas*).

In Portugal, the supreme tribunal of the Inquisition was in Lisbon. Inferior courts, established in other cities, were subject to it. A Grand Inquisitor was nominated by the king and confirmed by the Pope. After the independence of Portugal from Spain, John of Bragança wished to destroy the Inquisition, but succeeded only in depriving it of the right to confiscate the property of the condemned. For this, he was excommunicated after his death, and the queen was obliged to permit his body to receive absolution.

A king could compel the Inquisition to act according to some principles of justice. But it had an unanticipated influence on the state and on the moral character of the people. Noble and high-spirited people were more debased by its dark power than by any other instrument of arbitrary government, and the stagnation of intellectual life that followed it, even after the discovery of the New World, combined with other fatal causes to diminish the industry of the Iberian people, to weaken the power of the state, and to prevent, for a long time, progress to higher moral and intellectual development.

The horrible spectacle of the auto-da-fé

When the Inquisition pronounced a death sentence against an accused, it also ordered a holy *auto-da-fé* (act of faith)—a ritual of public penance.

This usually took place on a Sunday. At daybreak, the solemn sound of the cathedral's great bell called the faithful to witness the dreadful spectacle. Men of high rank pressed forward to offer their services in accompanying the condemned, who appeared barefooted, clothed in the dreaded *sanbenito*, with a conical cap (*caroza*) on their heads. The Dominicans, bearing the banner of the Inquisition, led the condemned on a procession. Directly after the monks came penitents who were to be punished by a fine. These were followed by the Cross, and after it the unfortunate wretches who had been condemned to death. Effigies of those who had fled, and the bones of the dead who had previously been condemned, were carried in black coffins, painted with flames and hellish forms, and the whole dreadful procession was followed up by monks and priests in the rear.

This procession went through the main streets of the city to the church, where a sermon was preached and the sentence pronounced. During this, the convicted stood before a crucifix, with an extinguished taper in their hands. As "the Church never pollutes herself with blood," when this ceremony was finished, a servant of the Inquisition gave each of those who had been sentenced a blow with the hand to signify that the Church no longer had any power over them and they had been abandoned (*relaxados*) to secular authorities. A civil officer, "who was affectionately charged to treat them kindly and mercifully,"[2] bound them with chains and led them to the place of execution, where they were asked in what faith they would prefer to die.

Those who chose to die as Catholics were strangled first.

---

[2] Amos Dean, *The History of Civilization*, vol. V (Albany, 1868), https://archive.org/stream/cu31924097890150/cu31924097890150_djvu.txt, 121.

The rest were burned alive. These *autos da fe*, or public burnings, were spectacles to which the people thronged as eagerly as to celebrations of military victory. Even kings considered it meritorious to be present with their courts and witness the victims' agonies. At the height of its power, between 1543 and 1684, the Portuguese Inquisition burned 1,379 people at the stake in public executions. So did the Inquisition proceed, during its most dreadful period of activity.

The Inquisition: A powerful obstacle to intellectual progress

The Inquisition annually published a catalogue of prohibited books, among which many excellent or innocent books were included along with those that were merely heretical or scandalous. Its unlimited authority even allowed it to search ships in harbour for books it disagreed with. All enlightened attempts to destroy the Inquisition, an antiquated instrument of a dark policy, proved without effect. The Inquisition went on aiming its terrors against people who were often guilty of nothing more than imprudence.

As the Spaniards took the Inquisition with them to America, so the Portuguese carried it to India, where they established it at Goa, and to Brazil. In the eighteenth century, the power of the Inquisition of Portugal was restrained by an ordinance that commanded the court to furnish its accused with the charges laid against them and the names of the witnesses, to allow the accused counsel, and to delay its sentences until the royal council could confirm them.

The last victim of the Inquisition, condemned to the flames, was a Jesuit priest. Finally, this macabre ecclesiastical organisation was abolished by the prime minister, the Marquis of Pombal, not only in Portugal, but also in Brazil and Goa, in 1761. The French had to wait another 47 years: Napoleon disbanded their Inquisition on 4 December 1808.

15. *When the gods became saints*

Christianity, which addresses the mind and the soul, excluded worship of more visible and sensual pagan deities. An invisible power replaced the idols that the early Celts, Greeks, and Romans had bowed before. The Christian saviour came to raise men from their knees and ask them to look to heaven and think of immortality. Faith and hope took the place of sacrifices; the vision was of a religion without temples or altars.

But imposing new faith upon the pagans was no easy task. The Christian god frequently proved insufficient to satisfy heathen hankerings for the divine. Pagan nations clung obstinately to their own gods, and to the pleasures of their sensual religions—their midnight processions and moonlit mysteries, and the worship of deities beyond number.

So it was that ancient superstitions were not subdued until the prudent Church of Rome put male and female saints in the niches that had once housed Lugh, Diana, and many others. They had turned the pagan gods into Catholic saints.

Today, Celtic pagan rituals can be traced back relatively easily to the Lusitanian ancestors of the Portuguese because Portugal remains one of the strongest followers of the Catholic Church, whose own rituals carry within them the traces of their pagan predecessors. The majority of Portuguese festivals are of Celtic origin, though the Catholic Church stigmatised these roots.

St Anthony and the Irish Nuadha Airgetlám

One of the strongest Celtic traces left in Portugal is the folklore concerning St Anthony. He is connected with the Irish figure Nuadha, who in Welsh is known as Nudd, and was given the epithet *Airgetlám*, meaning silver hand or arm. According to the Irish tale, Nuadha was a king of Ireland who, after having lost his arm in battle, stood down from his throne and gave his place to the mythological hero Lugh, who was to defend the country against invaders.

Lugh asked the people to donate broken pieces of silver so that the country's physicians and silversmiths could melt them down and make a silver arm for Nuadha so he could return to his throne, since according to the law, a king with a disability cannot be in command.

My father has told me that when he was a child, he would beg for silver coins in the name of St Anthony, at a place called *Braco de prata* (the silver arm). Though ostensibly the coins were for St Anthony, in reality the children were being cheeky: they might use the coins to buy lollies.

The silver coins, of course, relate to Lugh, and asking for them in the name of St Anthony was a metaphor for the ancient ritual of Nuadha Airgetlám, where Lugh asked the people for broken pieces of silver to make a silver arm to replace the one Nuada lost in the great battle at Mag Tuired. The ritual continued during my father's childhood, and today, in the city squares and markets of Lisbon, children still ask for silver coins to buy lollies and whatever else they desire.

The silver arm is also part of the story of the Maneta, the one-handed. An ancient Portuguese saying tells us that every broken piece goes to the one-handed *a Maneta*, whose story, the story of Nuadha, and the story of St Anthony, are one.[1]

St Anthony

The festival of St Anthony is part of the surviving Lusitano festival of Lugnasa (Lughnasadh in Irish Gaelic), and also relates to the festival of Hera, the goddess of marriage.

St Anthony (Portuguese: *Santo António*), born in Lisbon in 1195, is the patron saint of children, animals, and people who lose things, but one of his biggest roles is to help young people find spouses. In Spain, on St Anthony's birthday, the thirteenth of June, single women say to him: "*San Antonio bendito, solo te pido una bolas con plata y un buen marido*" ("Holy St Anthony, give me a purse full of silver and a husband"). In Lisbon, years ago, there was a custom of what were called the "weddings of St Anthony" (*casamentos do San Antonio*), where sometimes up to two hundred couples could get married. The couples that chose to marry on St Anthony's day all had their wedding ceremonies at the Sé Cathedral of Lisbon, which is near the house where Santo António was born. The whole of the wedding expenses of these couples were paid, and wedding gifts provided. Sometimes the sponsors of these events, which were often big industrial manufacturers, in cooperation with travel agents even offered the newlyweds a free honeymoon. Because of this, Santo António was given a nickname,

---

[1] St Anthony is connected to the Irish Nuadha because, as we see later in this chapter, according to Julius Caesar the Greek Hermes is related to Lugh or the Roman god Mercury. These are all the same figure in mythology and, as in Catholicism the gods became saints, the Greek Hermes became St Anthony.

"o casamentario"—the matchmaker.

My father tells me that St Anthony's festival on the thirteenth of June was a joyous occasion. Because St Anthony is the patron saint of Lisbon, on his day the whole city enthusiastically commemorates him. These festivities start on the twelfth of June—St Anthony's Eve—when young boys and girls dance around and jump over bonfires, and build altars in the saint's honour.

My father lived in a street called Sun Street, where for St Anthony's day, the residents made a large altar of wood, covered it with a white cloth, and decorated it with flowers, candles, and pictures of the saint. This was my father's excuse to go through the streets, begging for silver coins in his name.

St Anthony's sermon and the fintan

One of the famous stories of St Anthony is that at Rimini, having first attempted to preach to the townsfolk and found his words fell on deaf ears, was inspired to go to the beach and preach to the fishes. Seeing the fish throng to hear him, and then finally hearing the eloquence of his words, the heretics were at last converted.[2]

This seems a mere fiction, imagined by some Christian fabulist to reinforce the replacement by St Anthony of the Celtic tale of the *fintan*, the salmon of wisdom. This fish is the survivor of the great flood—while everybody else died, the *fintan* survived for many years. In Portuguese today, the root

---

[2]"St. Anthony Preaches to the Fishes," *Fish Eaters*, accessed 26 May 2016, http://www.fisheaters.com/animals9.html.

finta is often used in sporting terminology. For instance, *fintar un adversario* means to trick an opponent or take them by surprise. *Finta* is also a synonym of *driblar* (to dribble)—a term used in sports like soccer, basketball, handball, hockey and so on.

Preaching is a public discourse, on a religious subject or a piece of scripture. Homer saw Hermes as the patron of eloquence and the god of speech, and mentioned that the tongues of sacrificed animals were dedicated to him. Since we know St Anthony had the intelligence to deliver a sermon that even enthralled the fish, we may begin to see that he, Lugh, and Hermes or Mercury (messenger of the gods), are one and the same.

Lugh—Mercury—Hermes

According to Julius Caesar, Mercury was the god whom the Celts worshipped most. It seems the Romans had no regard for Celtic culture and often misunderstood the Celts' pantheon. However, Caesar wasn't an ordinary Roman: he was emperor of Rome, commanding chief of its army, and Pontifex Maximus of its pagan church—a title the Pope still uses in our day. Caesar was also a warrior, and fought the Celts himself. In fact, he was the conqueror of Gaul.

We know that in those days, warriors were also trained to become eloquent, and given Caesar's role as Pontifex Maximus, he must have had a fair knowledge of Celtic mythology as both the Celtic and Roman pagan traditions have the same roots in Indo-European culture. In fact, many Celtic scholars have agreed that Mercury and Lugh are one.

My father, a Lusitano, tells me that the highest mountain

range in Portugal, *A Serra a Estrela* (The Mountains of the Star, maximum height 1,993m) is what in Latin was called *Montes Herminius* (the mountains of Hermes). These mountains were the stronghold of the legendary Lusitanian Viriato against the Roman legions. Since my father's ancestors dedicated the highest mountain to the god Hermes, who is synonymous with Mercury, perhaps Caesar was right, and the Lusitanians venerated Mercury the most of all the gods.

But Hermes, who Homer said was the patron of eloquence, and who later writers make the inventor of letters, mathematics, weights, and measures, is also synonymous with Lugh. It is said that the Celts scrupulously never mentioned the names of their gods. Even in their religious oaths, they said, "I swear to the god to whom my tribe swears." After my father had translated the words of the Portuguese students' war cry from the ancient Celtic Lusitano dialect, he discovered a remarkable coincidence. The ancient Celtic god of wisdom and protector of the tribe—Lugh—had survived the upheaval of the turn to Christianity and was still the protector of the Portuguese students, especially of teams engaged in sporting competitions.

Chi ri be tata urra urra! (*urra*: hurrah)—these are the words of wild academic supporters cheering and backing up their teams. Curiously, nobody really knows what these words mean, but the students have an intense feeling, deep in their hearts and minds, for this magic phrases. Not even Coimbra University has shown any interest in translating what is of course an ancient European cry. Tata → tota → that → tout → tribe. Ri → king. Be → life. Urra (hurrah) → victory. Chi → cheer. The phrase, then, translates roughly to "Long life to the King—victory, victory, victory!" The phrase can be compared to the English phrases "God save the Queen," or "Long live the King."

"Ta ta" refers to the twin brothers of the sun; in Celtic mythology:

> There are two suns, summer and winter, bright and dark or stormy, and these are seen daily when the sun crosses the heavens bright, then sinks to the west darkening and remains dark through the night until dawn. The sun god therefore exists as twins—a bright twin and a dark twin. The god of the full year—the complete annual movement of the sun though the zodiac—is divided into its two half yearly parts—the good god, and his twin, the evil god. In solar mythology, the sun god has two twin sons.[3]

The saying *chi re be ta ta, urra urra urra* is not supposed to mention or refer to the god himself: in Celtic mythology it more respectful not to name him, so the saying can't be *Chi re be Lugh Lugh, urra urra urra*. In modern times, instead of saying "go with god" ("god be with ye" → "goodbye") in English we still use "ta ta". It is possible to call on the god of the tribe without mentioning his name.

Herminius or Lugh: The deity of seven trades

As we have already seen, after the gods became saints in Portugal, Lugh, who is also Hermes and Mercury, became St Anthony.

---

[3] Alkman, "Sun Gods as Atoning Saviours," *The Pagan Files*, 8 December 2006, http://alkman1.blogspot.com.au/2006/12/sun-gods-as-atoning-saviours.html.

Art has represented Mercury in various ways, first as the rude Hermes: in monuments of the more ancient style he appears with his beard just beginning to grow. In later periods, the prevailing representations of Hermes show a boy in the prime of youth and full power of early manhood. His dress consists of a short leather tunic, and in his left hand he bears a purse. Holding his right forefinger against his chin, he smiles archly at some private thought.

As a youth, we find Hermes represented in a variety of attitudes—sometimes with the purse in his hand, sometimes with the caduceus. In his beautiful and vigorous frame we see the inventor of gymnastics; in his attitude, air, and aspect, we see the prudence, cunning, and good nature of one who can easily win everybody over and accomplish anything. Artists made the rooster his symbol, on account of its vigilance and love of fighting (an allusion to gymnastics); but also the tortoise because of his invention of the lyre, which was made from a tortoise's shell; the purse because he was the god of commerce; the ram because he was the director of religious ceremonies and sacrifices; and the trunk of a palm tree, upon which his statues lean, because he was the inventor of arithmetic and writing upon palm leaves.

Celtic Druids and the Franciscan Orders

The Druids, or Celtic priests, had a well-known ritual they performed during the Lughnasadh festival. After the nocturnal swimming of the horses, they blessed the animals and hung their halters on an oak tree. The Franciscan Order, to which St Anthony of Lisbon belonged, was founded by St Francis of

Assisi in about 1210 AD, and still blesses horses and their halters on St Anthony's Day, the thirteenth of June. This pagan-cum-Catholic ritual is still performed in Padua, the Italian city where St Anthony was buried, and in Rome, by the Franciscan church, according to Italian folklore and customs.[4]

A halter is an arrangement of cords or straps placed around a horse's head to lead it or aid in confining it. *Halter* is also an archaic synonym for the noose used for hanging condemned people and, as *alter* in Portuguese, is an old word that survived in the language after the Latinisation of the country. In one Lusitanian territory, the Ribatejo (the banks of the River Tagus or Tejo) we find a horse breed called *O cavalo de Alter*, the sacred horse. In the 1970s, when my father still lived in Portugal, he had a four-wheel-drive motor vehicle, produced in Portugal, called the Alter. As we can see, the Portuguese selected a trademark for their car that named it after a special breed of native horse, as the Americans did with the Mustang.

The sacrifice of the head—of both humans and horses—was a tradition that went back to the roots of Indo-European civilisation. Both the Romans and Celts used to offer the head of a champion horse and used the blood for the lustral sacrifice. Again, we return to the famous scene in *The Godfather*.

Halter in Portuguese also means a weight lift.

> **Levantar o halter** To raise the weight. In this context, the word comes from a Latin root, *altus* (high), which itself has an Indo-European origin probably signi-

---

[4]Frances Toor, *Festivals and Folkways of Italy* (New York: Crown, 1953).

fying the sky or God, as in *Allah*, the Arab god.

Altar An elevated place intended for sacrifice.

At first, altars were made of stone or metal and were much adorned. They stood in the eastern part of the edifice, before the statue of the god, but lower. In a Catholic church, the altar is a table for the celebration of the Eucharist—a thanksgiving, the Lord's Supper, or Holy Communion. In this ritual, consecrated bread and wine stand in allegorically as Catholics eat the body of Jesus and drink his blood. This is connected with the ancient fertility rituals involving the killing of the king.

Hermes Trismegistus

The name Hermes Trismegistus was used by the Greeks to refer to a mythological person from ancient Egyptian tradition, who was said to have been the inventor of letters and all arts and sciences. The Egyptians called him Thoth, and placed his image alongside those of Osiris and Isis, who were his contemporaries. According to Diodorus, a Greek historian, Thoth was the friend and counsellor of the great Osiris. He formed the Egyptian language and invented the first written characters, and was the inventor of grammar, astronomy, arithmetic, geometry, music, and medicine. He was the first lawgiver, the founder of the Egyptians' religious ceremonies, the first cultivator of the olive tree and the first instructor in gymnastics and the joys of dance.

Sunchoniathon, Manetho, and Plutarch all give similar accounts of the wisdom of Thoth or Hermes Trismegistus. To transmit his knowledge to posterity, in these accounts, Hermes engraved it on pillars of stone, to which Plato and Pythagoras were supposedly indebted for much of their science. The inscriptions of Hermes were later copied into books, and a great number of books were ascribed to him. The school of Alexandria, in particular, attributed all its mystic sciences to him—magic, theosophy, alchemy and the like.

Some of the works ascribed to Hermes still exist, while we only have the titles of others. Among the first of those whose text remains is *Pomander and Asclepius* (London, 1628). Hermetic philosophy professes to explain all the phenomena of nature from the three chemical principles of salt, sulphur, and mercury. Everything related to Hermes is so uncertain and obscure that even the Egyptians the place where he came from cannot be ascertained with any certainty. It is for good reason that today the word *mercurial*, which relates to Hermes' Roman counterpart, means "sudden or unpredictable".

Scapegoat

A scapegoat is a person, often innocent, whom others blame for their problems. Often the scapegoat is something of a sacrificial victim: Jesus Christ can be seen as a scapegoat because he died to redeem his people from sin.

Scapegoats and the killing of kings are part of remote religious rituals. On New Year's Eve, the elders of a community would select a large, mature goat and lead it to the outskirts of their town. The people would gather around the goat and curse it as the cause of all their sins and ills. Then, once the Jewish chief priest had symbolically laid the people's sins upon it, the people would drive it into the wilderness with sticks and stones to prevent it coming back.

16. Heracles and Jesus Christ

The ancient Greeks used to crucify a man, incarnating Heracles, roast his body and then eat his flesh, believing that eating the flesh of a god was a thanksgiving—the god's supper. In the Catholic Church, sacraments are solemn ceremonies enjoined by Christ to be observed by his followers, in which their special relation to him is created or their obligations to him renewed and ratified. But the concepts of many Christian rituals are based on remote beliefs and ceremonies of the pagans, such as this one related to Heracles.

There are seven sacraments:

1. baptism
2. confirmation
3. the Eucharist
4. penance
5. extreme unction (anointing of the sick)
6. holy orders
7. marriage

The word *host*, used for the bread consecrated and eaten in the Catholic Eucharist, comes from the Latin *hostia* (sacrificial victim), which comes from the verb *hostire* (to strike). The host is a thin, circular portion of unleavened bread, and in this thanksgiving ritual, it is part of the Lord's Supper: Communion involves the consecration of bread and wine. When Catholic priests eat the host and drink the sacramental wine, which represent the body and blood of Jesus, it is an allegorical cannibal ritual related to ancient pagan ceremonies of fertility.

The ancients regarded the annual return of fertility—in which fertility became victorious over unfruitfulness—as the primary act of life. Because they believed that gods were guardians of cosmic power, to ensure a good crop they organised thanksgiving festivals. This form of thinking gave rise to the most important games of ancient Europe—the Capitoline Games, Lughnasadh, and the Ancient Olympics. These games were bound together by a common culture with remote Indo-European roots. They were rituals of thanksgiving for the first fruits of the harvest and simultaneously for the salvation of mankind.

17. Jesus Christ

Heracles—the king of the Romans' carnival—the king of the Celts' 'mardi gras'—the Greek pharmakoi—the scapegoat. All died for our salvation.

Natal invicto and Christendom

The unconquerable *natal*, a term coming from the Latin *natalis* and *natus* (to be born) is a festival for which Christ's rising from the dead is an allegory. Like the Greek Dionysus and the Celtic Cú Chulainn, Jesus gives an assurance that death does not end all, but rather that it is *birth* that is unconquerable. These figures are all sons of *Sol Invictus* (the unconquered sun).

As a result, today people who go to Church on Sunday are still heliolaters: Christians commemorate the birth of Christ, who in their belief is the saviour of the world, who died on the cross and then rose again for our salvation: just like the sun gods and other pagan figures. Though there have been billions of years since the creation of the world, according to Christian history it is only two thousand years ago that God sent his son to save us all. But in fact, all of the central concepts of Christian rituals are based on remote heathen beliefs. In pagan times, the king of the fertility rituals had to die on the cross, and men had been crucified for thousands of years before Jesus.

Fertility rites, king-killing, and dying gods

Crucifixion is the act of putting a man to death by nailing his hands and feet to a cross. Such a person is not necessarily a criminal, but could be a person bearing the sins of the people, which were laid on him by the hands of the high priest.

In our day, the modern kings of *Mardi Gras* and Carnival resemble the pagan kings of the ancient fertility rituals of the Greeks, Romans, and Celts. In Portugal, every year at the end of the third day of Carnival, the burial of the king is imitated. In our day, the modern kings of *Mardi Gras* and Carnival resemble the pagan kings of ancient Greek, Roman, and Celtic fertility rituals. In pagan times, the king involved in this fertility ritual actually had to die on the cross.

Air, fire, water, earth

The cross is a metaphor for the four indestructible elements of creation: air, fire, water, and earth. As a result, it symbolises permanence and the centre of the world—the crossroads. It is also a phallic symbol.

Saturnalia

The Roman festival of Saturnalia is equivalent to the Celtic Samhain, the modern Carnival, or Mardi Gras (meaning "Fat Tuesday"—the third day of the full moon). Saturnalia was a feast among the Romans, in commemoration of the happy period under the reign of Saturn, when freedom and equality prevailed, truth, confidence, and love united all, and violence and oppression were absent. It began at first as one day, then three, five, and finally, under the Caesars, it lasted seven days—from the seventeenth to the twenty-third of December.

The festival of Saturnalia began as soon as the woollen bands that had bound the feet of Saturn's statue throughout the year were removed, and at its commencement, a great number of wax papers were lit in the temple of Saturn as a sign that no more human victims were to be sacrificed. Slaves were freed from restraint during this season, wore caps as badges of freedom, and went about dressed in white togas and tunics adorned with purple. Masters and slaves changed places, and while the servants sat and banqueted at the tables, the masters and their guests waited upon them. Those masters who did not agree to this were obliged to submit to all sorts of ridiculous punishments. Some prisoners who dedicated their chains to Saturn were also set free.

Jests and freedom prevailed everywhere, and all ceased their various occupations. In the last days of the festival, which were added in later times, people sent presents to one another, particularly small images of gods called *sigilla* (seals). As a result, these days were sometimes called *Sigillaria*, and people were great-hearted and made acclamations of "Lo Saturnalia! Bona Saturnalia!"

Mardi Gras is a related festival. With its name referring to the third day of the full moon, it coincides with the killing of a king. The full moon is connected with unity and completeness, and is therefore the final phase of the fertility cycle: life–death–rebirth. Carnival, also related, takes its name from the

Latin *carnelevamen*, incorporating *carnis* (body) and *levamen* (solace). Together these roots mean "to cheer in grief or under calamity" or "to alleviate grief and anxiety."

There is a Portuguese saying that we have mentioned before, "*Rei morto, rei posto*," meaning that after the king dies he must be quickly replaced with a new one. In Portugal today, the Society of Recreation of the Philharmonic Pupils of Apollo still re-enacts this part of Carnival on the third day. Members of the society dress in fancy clothes and cry out lamentations while they carry a coffin in a procession along the streets of their suburb and visit other academies, including the Gremio, where my father attended primary school.

The word *philharmonic* is from the Greek words *philos* (loving) and *harmonia* (harmony), and as a whole means "loving harmony or music." Curiously, the society of the pupils of Apollo was founded at an address in a street of Arrábida, next to the primary school; later, it changed its location to the top of Sun Street. This is a remarkable coincidence given that Apollo was the sun god himself.

Why man had to die on the oak cross

As we have said, the cross is a metaphor for the four indestructible elements, and so it symbolises permanence and the centre of the world, or the crossroads. In ancient times, the cross had to be made of oak, because for the Greeks, Romans, and Celts, the oak was connected with the gods. Modern men, especially those living in big cities, are too busy to pay attention to nature, but in the past, men observed that during a thunderstorm the oak attracts more lightning than other trees, so they believed it was directly connected with the gods.

In modern times, to drive off a bad omen we still use the magical words, "touch wood." But with the passing of time, we forgot that for our wishes to come true, we must touch the oak, because only through that sacred tree can we touch the gods.

Pharmakoi

Our word *pharmacy* comes originally from the Greek word *pharmekeia* or *pharmakon*. Today, the art of preparing and compounding medicines, and dispensing them according to the prescriptions of doctors is called pharmacy. But in ancient times, *pharmakoi* were men who had to die for our salvation.

Greek settlers from the Island of Ionia founded the ancient colony of Olisippo, now Lisbon, in 600 BC. They brought from their Greek island the festival of Thargelia, which involved the rite of expelling two men, known as *pharmakoi*, who were sent into the wilderness bearing the sins of the people, which were laid upon them by the hands of the high priest. Made to bear the blame for others, they were stoned, beaten, and killed for the salvation of the tribe.

Heracles

The Greek Heracles or Alcides bore a resemblance to the figure of Jesus. Although indeed a man, the hero has a godlike portion of his nature, which is divine in origin, as he is the son of the king of the gods by a mortal mother. His indomitable perseverance gives him victory, while his death secures him immortality and a seat among the gods. After death, Heracles was carried up to heaven, and his friends were unable to find his bones or ashes. They showed their gratitude to his memory by raising an altar, and his worship soon became as universal as his fame.

Heracles is the most celebrated hero of the mythological age of Greece, in whom poetry presented a model of human perfection according to the ideals of the heroic age. In him, the highest bodily vigour united with the finest qualities of heart and mind and was devoted to mankind's welfare. His nature was to strive perpetually after divine excellence, but under the common conditions of humanity—amid a ceaseless succession of labours and sacrifices—and it was his indomitable persever- ance that gave him victory.

What story could be more interesting and instructive than that of Heracles, presenting as it does a clear picture of human life with its alternations of fortune and struggle, and its hopes and prospects? It is no wonder that Heracles has become a fa- vourite subject of poets and artists, who have multiplied his achievements.

The birth of Heracles was attended by many miraculous and supernatural events. He was brought up by Tirynthus or, according to Diodorus, at Thebes, and before he was eight months old the jealous Juno, who was intent on his destruc- tion, sent two snakes to devour him.

The child Heracles, fearless before these serpents, boldly seized them in both his hands and squeezed them to death while his brother Iphicles alerted the house with his frightful shrieks.

Zeus sought to protect his favourite son in every way, and to make him worthy of immortality. Once, while Juno was sleeping, he laid the infant Heracles on her breast to suck the milk of the goddess and imbibe immortality. Early on, he was instructed in the liberal arts and Castor, the son of Tyndarus, taught him how to fight. He was taught by Erytus how to shoot with bow and arrows, by Autolycus to drive a chariot, by Linus to play the lyre, and by Eumolpus to sing. Like the rest of his illustrious contemporaries, he became the pupil of the centaur Chiron, and under him Heracles perfected himself and became the most valiant and accomplished hero of his age.

When he had completed boyhood, he retired to a solitary district and stood at the meeting of two ways, reflecting on his fate. Two lovely female figures approached, and one, Pleasure, invited him to follow her flowery path. The other, Virtue, invited him to choose a course full of labour and self-control, but crowned with honour and immortality. Virtue prevailed, and Heracles resolved to follow her guidance without shrinking.

He accompanied the Argonauts to Colchis before delivering himself to the kind of Mycenae. He helped the gods in their wars against the giants, and through him alone Zeus attained victory. He killed Laomedon and pillaged Troy. When Iole—the daughter of Eurytus, king of Echalia—with whom he was deeply enamoured, refused his entreaties, he became prey to a second fit of insanity and murdered Iphitus, the only one of Eurytus's sons who had favoured his suit to Iole.

After some time, Hercules was purified of the murder and his insanity ceased, but the coldness with which the Pythia received him irritated him, and he resolved to plunder Apollo's temple and carry away the sacred tripod. Apollo opposed him, and a serious conflict began that nothing but the interference of Zeus with his thunderbolts could prevent.

The oracle told Heracles that he must be sold as a slave and stay three years in the most abject servitude to recover from his malady. He complied, and Hermes, by order of Zeus, conducted him to Omphale, queen of Lydia, to whom he was sold. In Lydia, he cleared the country of robbers, and Omphale, astonished by the greatness of his exploits, restored his freedom and married him. According to some, Heracles had Alegaus and Lamon by Omphale, and from this pairing Croesus, later king of Lydia, was descended. In Lydia, Heracles also had Alceus by one of Omphale's female servants that he was enamoured with.

After his years of slavery were completed, Heracles returned to the Peloponnesus, where he re-established himself on the throne of Sparta Tyndarus, who had been expelled by Hippocoon. He became one of Dejanira's suitors and married her after overcoming all his rivals. He had to leave Calydon, his father-in-law's kingdom, because he inadvertently killed a man with a blow of his fist, and on account of that expulsion he was not present at the hunting of the Calydonian boar.

From Calydon, Heracles went to the court of Ceyx, the king of Trachinia. On his way, he was stopped by the swollen streams of the Evenus, where the centaur Nessus attempted violence to Dejanira under the pretence of carrying her over the river.

Heracles perceived Dejanira's distress and killed the centaur, who, as he died, gave her his tunic, which had the power to recall a husband from infidelity. Ceyx received Heracles and his wife with great marks of friendship, and purified him of the murder he had committed at Calydon.

Heracles still remembered he had once been refused the hand of Iole, and made war against her father, Eurytus, killing him and three of his sons. Iole then fell into his hands, finding that Heracles loved her as much as before, and went with him to Mount Oeta, where he planned to raise an altar and make a solemn sacrifice to Zeus. As he did not have the proper tunic in which to offer a sacrifice, he sent Lichas to Dejanira to obtain one.

Learning of her husband's attachment to Iole, Dejanira sent Heracles the tunic she had received from Nessus, but it was poisoned with the venom of the Lernaean Hydra, and as soon as Heracles put it on he was overcome by a desperate distemper and found that the toxin had penetrated his bones. Though he tried to pull the tunic off, it was too late, and amid pain and torture, he implored Zeus to give him his protection, gave his bow and arrows to Philoctetes, and erected a large pyre on top of Mount Oeta. He spread the skin of the Nemean lion on the pyre and laid himself on it as though on a bed, leaning his head on his club.

According to some Philoctetes, or to others Paean or Hyllus, was ordered to set fire to the pyre, and the hero found himself suddenly surrounded by flames, but showed neither fear nor astonishment. Zeus saw him from heaven, and told the gods around him that he would raise to the sky the immortal parts of this hero who had cleared the earth of so many monsters and tyrants. The gods applauded Zeus's resolution, and the burning pile was suddenly surrounded by dark smoke as the fire consumed the mortal parts of Heracles. Then he was carried to heaven in a chariot drawn by four horses, with loud thunderclaps signalling his elevation. His friends, who could find neither his bones nor his ashes, showed their gratitude to his memory by raising an altar where the pyre had stood.

Menoetius, the son of Actor, offered Heracles the sacrifice of a bull, a wild boar, and a goat, and encouraged the people of Opus to observe the same religious ceremonies yearly. The worship of Heracles soon became as universal as his fame, and he received many surnames and epithets from places where his worship was established or from the labours he underwent. His temples were numerous and magnificent, and his divinity revered. The ancients held him up as a true model of virtue and piety—since his whole life had been employed for the benefit of mankind, he was deservedly rewarded with immortality.

What is the origin of this story of Heracles? Many writers believe that the oriental deities whom the Greeks identify with Heracles are merely astronomical symbols. According to Herodotus and Diodorus, the Egyptian Heracles belongs to the twelve great heavenly deities who sprang from the eight gods 17,000 years before Amasis. Since these eight gods, as well as the twelve, have astronomical roots, some believe that Heracles is merely the symbol of the course of the sun through the twelve signs, or through a year. The fable that he lived 17,000 years before Amasis, then, signifies that men have been making astronomical calculations from that time.

The Phoenician Heracles, whose proper name is Melcarthas, appears to have a similar origin, given the name of his mother, Asteria (the starry heavens). It is believed that even in the Theban or Grecian Heracles, many traces of his oriental, astronomical origins are to be found. In this idea, Heracles' twelve labours signify the sun's passage through the signs of the Zodiac. His marriage with Hebe was explained by the ancients as a symbol of the renewal of his course after its completion.

We must remember that the Greek Heracles is of Phoenician origin, and that his native city, Thebes, was a Phoenician colony. The Phoenician Heracles, as the patron and symbol of the nation, accompanied his people wherever they went and settled. Thus, the travels of Heracles appear as a symbol of Phoenician extension by commerce and navigation, and of the civilisation that was a consequence of it.

It is possible that no Heracles ever existed, and then we must consider that the Heraclides are merely descendants of the Greco-Phoenician colony of Thebes. But a Theban Heracles may well have existed, and this seems probable because of an old tradition that the name of Heracles the man was not originally Heracles at all, but Alcaeus, and that he took his divine name from the god.

Jesus: Jew or Celt?

Everything in the story of Jesus Christ is part of a prehistoric tradition.

Apart from his appearance—he is always portrayed as having white skin, blonde hair and bright blue eyes, many things about Christianity show that it is not an original system of ideas. In fact, the Jews never accepted Jesus as the Messiah because every detail of his story was part of a remote sacrificial tradition—that of the Tammuz cult. Dionysus, Attis, Adonis, Tammuz, Jesus, Heracles, and Cú Chulainn are all one. All are born of a virgin, and are blond-haired solar heroes. Cú Chulainn, the Celtic Christ, is the son of the sun god, Lugh.

Jesus's resurrection represents the victory of the new solar god over the old year. In the same way that my father thanks the orientals for the preservation of Celtic martial arts, we must admit that thanks to Christianity, Celtic mythology is still very much alive today.

According to one early Jewish story, the real father of Jesus was a soldier in the Roman army, a native of Gaul called Tiberius Julius Pantera. If this was the case, Jesus could indeed have had Celtic blood. But we must admit that his philosophy was far from that which prevailed in the Celtic realm. Barbara G. Walker writes:

> Clement of Alexandria said every woman should be filled with shame by the thought that she is a woman, and quoted Jesus' words from the Gospel According to the Egyptians: "I have come to destroy the works of the female."[1]

The truth, I think, is that Jesus could never have said such nonsense. In fact, we know that everything in the Gospels was fabricated and distorted. But if Jesus had denounced women in this way, he could not have been a Celt. Yet, there are other hypotheses about Jesus's origins related to Pantera, which connect him with the god of wine, Dionysus, lover of the panther.

The Magdala temple and The Passion of the Christ

Looking the Mel Gibson film *The Passion of the Christ*, with the aid of Babylonian, Celtic, and Greek mythology, we can see that the scenes interpret far more ancient myths than those of Jesus's time.

The film starts with Jesus very disturbed and hiding in the woods away from the temple soldiers until Judas gives his

---

[1] Barbara G. Walker, *Belief and Unbelief.*

secret place away. After Jesus is arrested, he is whipped and suffers the torment of carrying the cross to Calvary. As we watch the film, we feel sorry for him, and there is a question we must all have in our minds. Why would Jesus want to carry the cross? Why does he keep holding onto it?

The reason may be that Jesus at first began to run away, but after his arrest, he accepted his fate and decided to die on the cross. Those who have seen the film might have noticed a strange creature holding a baby with an old face in one scene. To understand what's going on here we must go back once again to Babylonian mythology, where we find Nimrod (aka Ninus), the lord of Babylon and the sun god. His consort was Semiramis, who was also the priestess of his cult. She gave birth to a son called Tammuz, and declared that the child was her deceased husband, the god, reborn. Then she became the mother and wife of the god, and an independent cult developed around her.

Sacred prostitution at the temple of Magdala

At different times in history, many misguided philosophers and fanatical sects have preached against women. Such a violation of the order of nature has survived in our times, particularly in Arab countries, which were once, probably, not as restrictive as at present.

It was once customary for every woman in Babylon, once in her life, to give herself up to any stranger who came for her, in the temple of the goddess of love. In Syria and other countries of Western Asia, girls served for several years in the temple of the Asiatic Aphrodite, and bestowed their favours on visitors to the temple. In India and other countries of the subcontinent, the first enjoyment of a woman immediately after her marriage belonged to the Brahmins. This connection with the priests was even sought after through the offering of prayers and gifts.

Mary of Magdala and Mary Magdalene

According to the Church, Mary Magdalene was cured by Christ of an inveterate disease, and proved her gratitude by her devoted adherence to him. She served him with her property, attended him on his journeys, and wept at his crucifixion. She was the last to leave his grave, and the first to behold him risen.

The history of her conversion from a licentious life was confounded with the story of Mary of Magdala, and so the ideal of St Magdalene was formed, which gave occasion to some of the most celebrated artworks in history. Penitent women who had lead licentious lives banded together early on and established a religious order under the saint's protection, which existed in Germany before 1215. Similar institutions arose about the same time in France, Italy, Spain, and Portugal.

Mary of Magdala was so named after a city on the lake of Galilee, which was known as the village of doves. It was conquered by the Roman general Vespasian at the time of Emperor Nero, around 67 AD, and was famous for its wealth and moral corruption. In Magdala there was a temple of sacred prostitution.

Mary Magdalene, on the other hand, is by an old, erroneous interpretation the sinner mentioned in *Luke 7*, where her name is not given, who Jesus assured that her sins would be forgiven because of her repentance and her trust in him. In reality, she may have been a priestess of the temple of Magdala, where the sacred marriage involving the ritual coition of the king with a priestess took place.

The Sumerian ritual of sacred prostitution passed to Greece; Strabo mentions that there were a thousand sacred prostitutes at the temple of Aphrodite in Corinth, where the Isthmian Games were held. He tells us that there was even an ancient Greek word, *korinthiazomai* (Corinthianise), that meant to fornicate.

It seems that the crucifixion of Christ was a substitute for the sacred marriage between Christ and Mary Magdalene, which would have been a sexual ritual comparable to the Dionysian festival or the Celtic Beltane. From Greek authors, we know that during the ritual of Dionysus, brides-to-be were flogged. Flagellation was related to fertility rituals and was also a sexual stimulant. At the same time the cross could be a phallic symbol; in parallel, the Dionysian cult was a social outlet for releasing sexual tension, and used wine to lift inhibitions. Dionysian and Beltane rituals were both practiced at night, away from cultivated fields, and the preference was for high locations.

As Dionysus is related to Apollo, the sun god, so is Cú Chulainn related to Lugh, the Celtic sun god. Both Dionysus and Cú Chulainn are lords and saviours.

The Passion

Observing *The Passion of the Christ* once again, we can see how it interprets the ancient Sumerian rituals, as though the Passion is a sacred marriage in which the bridegroom, Jesus, goes to his nuptials. He comes to the marriage bed of the cross, and mounting it, he consummates the marriage. The cross represents the phallus, while the three women in the story: Mary his virgin mother; Mary Magdalene; and the crone, Mary's mother, the grandmother of Jesus, are the three goddesses who preside over the sun god's death.

Jesus is nailed to a living tree, representing the tragedy of cyclical life: we are born–we live–we die. Inspired priests chose Christ to die as a substitute king in a violent execution on the tree of life, which is at once the instrument of death and a representation of the virile phallus. The old king dies and, being resurrected, becomes the new king.

The raven was considered a messenger from the underworld to those who were doomed to die in battle, and *The Passion of the Christ* shows us a scene where a raven pokes out the eyes of a man crucified beside Christ, because he was furious and never ceased cursing and swearing. Since he could not see what was happening—the momentous ritual sacrifice—the raven took out his eyes. For the Church, the raven is a symbol of penance.

Morrígan: the Celtic triple goddess

The three goddesses of destiny who appear in the ritual sacrifice of the king are a feature of many civilisations around the world, so it is no surprise that we find them in Greek and Celtic mythology.

The Celtic festival of Beltane was designed to promote the healthy growth of the harvest and the human population. Married women who were unable to become pregnant with their husband were even encouraged, during Beltane, to go into the woods and try another man. The "bride of Christ", Mary Magdalene, is portrayed by the Catholic Church as a prostitute, but

234

we can understand that in fact she was a priestess of the Magdala temple and that the "profane" rituals of Beltane commemorated the sacred marriage on which the fertility of the land depended.

The Catholic Church teaches that Mary was still a virgin when she conceived Jesus, not by sexual relations but through a miracle involving the Holy Spirit. But the ancients also had another interpretation of the story of immaculate conception, which makes more sense. In this tradition, Mary or her equivalent is an independent goddess, and is not dependent on the father god—she is a virgin with an independent cult.

To see more of what the virgin symbolises in ancient beliefs, we can compare the Celtic belief in the triple goddess Morrígan with the modern cult of Our Lady of Fatima, who appeared in Portugal. During times of great difficulty, the Portuguese are still deeply connected to the great mother goddess, especially through the cult of Mary of Fatima, which is a modern fabrication of the Portuguese Catholic Church. But like the ancient cult of the goddess, the cult of Fatima has considerable independence from the traditions of the father god, and is in reality even stronger than it. During the colonial war, Mary achieved the fantastic miracle of filling the coffers of the Church with incredible riches.

The war goddess

When confronted with dangerous situations, Portuguese soldiers all ask for Mary's protection. Their mothers also promised thanksgiving to her when their sons returned from war. Today, Mary still generates massive amounts of money for the Church and, as in ancient times, what is left over when expenses have been covered goes to the chief priests and temple staff.

Fatima is something of a Trojan Horse for the Church, used to smuggle goddess worship into Catholic traditions, and it creates an ambiguity in mainstream Christianity. Acting as a surrogate for Jesus and God the father, she exercises a great deal of authority. The fortune that she generates for the Church also assures her total independence, as does her lack of need for a male partner, as a virgin.

Though the Church knows Mary holds this incredible power, it refuses to accept this reality. They attempt to persuade the people that she is only a mediator between God and the people. But those who claim her protection often believe that she—the goddess—is omnipotent. Worship of Mary gave rise to a belief in the miraculous power of several old images of the virgin. At Loreto in Italy, and at Częstochowa in Poland, there are images celebrated for their powers to heal diseases of both mind and body. Catholics have long been accustomed to perform pilgrimages to obtain indulgences promised by papal bulls, and today they are as likely to make pilgrimages to seek favours from the virgin—from the goddess.

Catholic persecution of the Jews

In Portugal, my father used to get expelled from Catholic religious classes because of his impertinent questions. He tells me that, like a lot of people, he couldn't understand why the Church prosecuted and burned so many Jewish people when Jesus was a Jew himself. But Jesus, like John the Baptist, died as a scapegoat for the sins of others and to preserve the earth's fertility. Because of a distorted interpretation of such ancient rituals, the Jews, God's "chosen people", have been persecuted in the name of the God that is supposed to protect them. For instance, in Bavaria in 1348, 12,000 Jews perished in the holy fires of the Catholic Church, and after the Second World War, the Vatican organised a sophisticated network that helped Nazi war criminals escape to South America. The Church even supplied them with forged paperwork. Perhaps it is not too ironic that two powerful names in Church history are linked to mass murders.

Torquemada

The torc or torque is the symbol of Celtic freedom. But Torquemada (1420–1498 AD) was the evil man behind the Catholic Spanish Inquisition. Similarly, *innocent* means "free of moral corruption" or "not guilty of a crime", but Pope Innocent, who served from 401–417 AD, said that God gave the Church the right to kill. In fact, the history of the Church has always involved forgery, dictatorship, and extreme violence. It always gets along with and supports dictators, fascists, and mafiosi.

The absurdity of all this is that it is done in the name of Jesus, who was himself a pacifist. Christ, like Buddha or Gandhi, wanted to achieve peace not by violence but through dialogue. We must admit that priests are like politicians: we no longer expect them to keep their word or tell the truth.

Christian Churches supposedly stand as a testament to men's admiration for Jesus. But Jesus preached in open spaces and criticised the organised religion of his time. So in the name of a man who was against materialism, fortunes have been spent on churches, many wars have been waged, and people have been murdered because they didn't follow Christian dictates.

What did Christ himself teach? He was against superfluous things. He observed and denounced how his religion (Judaism) did business, and as a result, its leaders allowed him to be sacrificed. We don't need to see a film to understand the truth, but by watching *The Passion of the Christ*, we can see a dramatisation of how it was the Jewish priests, far more than the Romans, who wanted Jesus dead.

The Romans couldn't have cared less if Jesus was the king of the Jews. Pontius Pilate only became scared of him when the leading rabbis accused Jesus of telling his followers not to bow to Caesar and promised to report it to Rome if Pilate didn't do something about it. He then had no choice but to condemn Jesus to death.

The Jewish religious organisation then used Jesus to fulfil its annual sacrifice. In the end, at least according to the film, after the temple guards had arrested Jesus, he decided to accept his role in the sacrifice and be killed for the salvation of his people. It is for Jesus' devotion to others' welfare that we love him, not just as God but also as one of us. He lived like a free man pursuing the values also held by Celtic culture.

18. Catholic and pagan gods

Father Acácio Marques is an illustrious Catholic priest who has dedicated himself to the rejuvenation of the Catholic Church for more than twenty years. Thanks to his excellent knowledge of theology, he has become a well-known journalist in Portugal, and as a result the Portuguese chaplain of Sydney invited him to Australia to preach to Portuguese migrant communities. Below is an article of his from 19 August 1998, which offers thoughts on important topics:

> Each person has a vision and my vision of the Portuguese migration phenomenon is not only the search for a better life but also behind that is God. Because in reality God is the conductor of the people's history and the history of each one, in this case the Portuguese. Portugal has a mission to accomplish in the world, called the fifth spirit. God takes advantage of the Portuguese migration phenomenon to take his name to places and people far from Portugal, in this case Australia.

> The Portuguese are conscious of their mission in the world but [are] also attached to Christianity. It is from experience, and according to the books, that for them to be able to advance and for the existence of progress in everything nothing can make progress without going to the root. Therefore it is important that the Portuguese go back to their roots to accomplish their mission in the

world. Everything they did they have done perfectly, but the Council of Vaticano Segundo [Vatican II] tells us that 2,000 years have gone past and we must go back to the beginning of the Church which is to be Christian.

After an exhortation inviting the Portuguese to a long-awaited realisation, full of faith, Father Acácio finished by telling the Portuguese that God took advantage of his articles written in newspapers to bring him to Australia to tell the Portuguese to be good, and to be Catholics, and always to remember that Portugal grew up under the protection of the Catholic Church.

My father's mission

According to a famous theologian who specialised in the science of Christian divinity, God took advantage of the Portuguese to propagate the gospel, in Australia and in many other countries of the world. But my father's Lusitanian gods sent him to Australia to learn that the Catholic Church usurped the religious festivals of his ancestors, and then to tell the world.

This respected Portuguese theologian says we must go to the country's origins to find the truth. But in Portugal, my father could never find the facts of history, because the Inquisition burned so many books and people. Portuguese history books are still missing the pages burned by the holy fires of ignorance.

Everything the Church has done for nearly 2,000 years, it has done with conviction. Here we have a huge contradiction, although the Pontifex Maximus of the Catholic Church, the Pope, has asked forgiveness for the past crimes of the Church more than a hundred times, Father Acácio, whose words you see above, has forgotten the holocaust the Inquisition brought upon mankind. If we go to its roots, we see that the Inquisition was comparable to the Nazis of modern times.

We must ask a sacramental question: if there is only one God, who sent my father to Australia on his holy mission? In 1896 we had the first modern Olympic Games. Half a century later, my father was born. My great-grandmother told my grandfather to call his son (my father) Ivo, because one day it was believed he would bring an important message to his people.

A century after the rebirth of the modern Olympics, the Lusitanian gods sent my father to Australia to fulfil my great-grandmother's prediction and tell the Portuguese that their ancestors had staged more important games than those of the Greeks, which extended to the rest of the Europe because they were Celtic festivals.

The reason people do not learn about this in Portugal is that the Catholic Church doesn't want the Portuguese to know that its rituals and festivals were usurped, and had first belonged to our Celtic ancestors, the Lusitanos.

Christian contempt for pagan rituals

If we examine the relationship it bears to different religions, it is clear that Christianity is guilty of sacrilege. When confronted with much older rituals, as a precaution pagans always left ancient religions alone, showing great intellectual wisdom. On the other hand, Christians acted contemptuously towards the old religions, showing no practical wisdom. To impose their faith, they ravaged temples and broke sacred images of the pagan gods, using blasphemous language against pagan religious opinions and customs of worship.

After severe testing and the failure of these methods of converting the pagans, the Church put the gods back in their niches, adapted pagan rituals and covered everything with a Christian veneer, in a careful plan to win Christian devotion from the heathens.

It is true that Portugal grew up under the protection of the Catholic Church. But it is also true that the Church usurped the Lusitanos' religious rituals. Portuguese academics indiscriminately made the word *Lusitano* synonymous with *Portuguese.* But saying every Portuguese is Lusitano is like saying every Australian is Aboriginal, or Anglo-Saxon.

It would be more correct to say that every Lusitano is Portuguese, but not every Portuguese person is Lusitano. To be a Portuguese citizen does not make one Lusitano.

Race A class of people who have sprung from common stock. A tribe.

Citizen A native of a city or a country, or an inhabitant who enjoys the freedom and privileges of the city or country he resides in.

Nation A people inhabiting a territory and united by common political institutions.

Os jogos: The games

There is an old saying in Portuguese that you cannot run from a place you are destined to go to...

In 1996, in the City of Hume, Victoria, Australia, my father symbolically recreated the ancient Isthmian Games. The experience my father and I have had with the magic of this kind of festival goes back to my father's neighbourhood upbringing in the heart of the Portuguese capital, which is as old as history itself. The games that animated the children on the Street of the Sun are the surviving traces of the old festivities of the Celtic civilisation, mingled with pagan Roman and probably Jewish rituals, all of which had survived in some form the ordeals of the new law and faith—Christianity.

The revelations in this book will surprise many people, which is understandable, considering that the fanatics of the Portuguese Inquisition were so fond of burning books, especially the ones that spoke of earlier religions and faiths.

After collecting information from the Victorian State Library, my father realised that the Lisbon suburb where he grew up was a sacred place to our ancestors. Armed with copies of books that had, in Portugal, perished in the "holy fire," and hence the pages ripped out of Portuguese history, my father and I have been able to read into the past and reconstruct our country's true history.

The first surprising thing we discovered is that our surname is connected to the place where my father was born. The whole suburb was rebuilt in an area that had been destroyed by a strong earthquake, which devastated the city of Lisbon in the year 1755. Nevertheless, in breathing the ambrosial odour typical of a sacred place, we can still raise the memory of mystical, pagan times that probably had the same grandeur as Olympus, if not in beauty then at least in spiritual strength.

Indeed, Olympia and the place where my father was born both suffered the same fate. They were occupied by the Roman legions; they were invaded by barbarian tribes; their traditions were suppressed by the new faith of the Christians; and finally an earthquake destroyed them.

Coincidence or fate?

Rato is the Latinised name that comes from the ancient Gaelic *rath* or *rathu*, which is anglicised as *rathouse*, or town hall, from the German *Rathaus*. All over Europe we find *rathus* surviving mainly inside medieval castles. These were in fact Celtic round fortresses made of wood and earth. Correspondingly, Ratis was the ancient British Goddess of the fortress. As Re was the Irish goddess of the moon and night, so Ra was the great god of Egypt, lord of the sun and sky. The *rathu* or *rathouse*, then, was the house of the sun god, and this is what our name signifies.

Observing a *rathu* place (*a praça do rato*), we can easily understand that the space was sacred to the ancient pagans, because of the number of Catholic churches we can find in such an area today. The common practice, following the rise of Christianity, was to replace the heathen temples with the new churches. An example of this is the Vatican Hill, which, according to a Vatican curator, "takes its name from the Latin word *Vaticanus, a vaticiniis ferendis*, in allusion to the oracles, or *Vaticinia*, which were anciently delivered [t]here."[1]

One remarkable habit we have noticed when visiting some historical *rathus* in Poland is that the Poles still keep roosters (weathervanes) on top of them, a habit that in Portugal was transferred to the top of the church tower (*campanario*), because in that country the *rathus* were destroyed, and only the name and the place survived. Today, Sun Street at the *rato* is *Rua do Sol ao Rato*—once, "the door of the sun." The reader can understand why the street was given the sun's name—every castle in Portugal has a "sun door" (*porta do sol*). But in case you believe this is pure coincidence, consider this, everyone who walks from the *rato*, up Sun Street, will find himself in *Campo de Ourique*—the Camp of the Oracle.

Campo de Ourique

The Camp of the Oracle, or the Oracle Field, was an ancient oracular place at the time when Celts, Romans, and Jews lived together and shared religious beliefs and rituals. This suburb was rebuilt in an area still called "the Earthquakes", which remembers the severity of the Great Lisbon Earthquake of 1755. Two and a half centuries later, it still bears the "shaking name." In fact, in Campo de Ourique there is a police station called the Police Station of the Earthquakes (*A esquadra da Policia dos Terramotos*).

---

[1] Cav. H. J. Massi, *Compendious Description of the Museums of Ancient Sculpture, Greek and Roman, in the Vatican Palace, Third Edition* (Rome: Vatican Typography, 1889), 7.

Ourique A morbid place. Also *ouric*. A variant of *uric*. The Latin *uria* is derived from the Greek *ouria*. The *ur* or *our* in *ourique* is the same as the *ur* in urine.

Uric acid A crystallised acid found in the urine of humans, certain animals, reptiles, and birds, produced in the metabolism of nitrogenous bodies and excreted by the kidneys. Uric acid stones have a yellowish or reddish-brown colour.

Autopsy From the Greek *autos*, meaning *self*. The word *autopsy* is from this root; it is an observation one makes oneself.

Though *autopsy* is now usually synonymous with postmortem examination, the ancient priests were already thoroughly familiar with autopsies. Roman priests, Jewish prophets, and Celtic Druids all foretold events by observing the entrails of sacrificed animals and men. The auspices, whose name comes from the Latin *auspicium* and *auspex*, meaning "one who looks at birds,"[2] were introduced to Rome by Romulus, who brought them from Etruria. They enjoyed their authority until the time of Constantine, who was the Roman emperor from 306 to 337 AD and prohibited all mind-reading on pain of death. At that time there had been seventy auspices, and their chief priest was called Sumrnus.

---

[2]Wikipedia contributors, "Augury," *Wikipedia, The Free Encyclopedia*, http s://en.wikipedia.org/w/index.php?title=Augury&oldid=720051474 (accessed May 29, 2016).

The aruspex, or Magister Publicus, and the oracles of the Greeks

This section is about the utterances given by people who pretend to be divinely inspired, and about the places where these pronouncements took place in certain ceremonies.

The Latin equivalent of our word *oracle* is *oraculum*, which comes from *oro*, meaning to speak or pray, and from *os* or *oris* (the mouth). *Oral, orifice, orator*, and even *adore*, are all related words. *Oracle* can mean many things: the answer of a god or an inspired priest or priestess, to a question posed about some affair; the deity who gave or was supposed to give answers to such questions; the place where they were answered; the sanctuary; a divine communication, revelation, or message; or a person known for being uncommonly wise, whose opinions had great weight.

There is insufficient trustworthy information from antiquity to determine the origin of the oracles. The Egyptian oracles date from a period where little evidence even of the prevailing traditions can be found, let alone historical monuments or much writing. The oldest of these was at Meroe, and then those of Thebes and Ammonium. In each of these places, Ammon was the presiding deity. The oracle at Dodona, the oldest in Greece, was formed on the model of Ammon, but united an Egyptian and Pelasgian character.

Herodotus's account of the origin of the Pelasgian oracle shows that a colony from Africa attempted, by its institution, to establish itself in Greece. Consecrated women from Africa—prophetesses, the black doves of Herodotus—dedicated this oracle to Ammon.

The oracle of Boeotia was perhaps of equal antiquity. It first belonged to the earth, then to Themis, and was later transferred to Apollo. The oracle at Delphi came later, but became the most famous of all, partly because of its connection with the council of the Amphictyons at Pylae.

Zeus had further oracles at Elis, Pisa, and in a cave beneath the earth in Crete. Apollo had oracles at Delos, where trees whispered answers to queries; at Claro, not far from Colophon, where a consecrated river inspired the priests; and in many other places.

In addition to all these, the oracles of Trophonius at Lebadeia and of Amphiaraus at Oropus, on the borders of Attica and Boeotia, were also highly regarded in Greece. Juno had an oracle in the Corinthian territory, and Heracles had one at Bura in Achaea, where answers were given by throwing dice. Bacchus had an oracle at Amphicleia in Phocis, which returned answers in dreams. The Byzantine poet John Tzetzes mentions an oracle of Ulysses or Odysseus, and other heroes and prophets had theirs.

The Romans had few oracles of their own; there were the Albunea, the Cumaean Sibyl, the Sibylline books, and the oracle of Faunus and Fortuna at Praeneste, which belonged to the earliest times and later lost its reputation. Otherwise, they consulted the oracles of Greece and Egypt.

Oracles were consulted and precious gifts presented to them in all cases of great moment or necessity—at the founding of cities and colonies, the introduction of new governments, and the undertaking of important enterprises of war and peace. The priests of these oracles needed to exercise great watchfulness and prudence to avoid undermining their own authority, and opaqueness and ambiguity in their answers were their typical recourse. Still, there were obvious failures of divination and prophecy. Even so, and in spite of well-known instances where oracles were corrupted, they long maintained their standing. Only under the reign of the Roman emperor Theodosius the Great, who reigned from 347 to 395 AD, were the temples of the deities the oracles favoured closed or demolished.

19. Oracles and omens

Ourique–oracle–omen

Omen From the Latin *omen*, from *oris* (the mouth). Also connected with *auris* (the ear). An event or occurrence thought to predict good or evil; a prognostication.

Ourique A place of divine prognostication, named after the colour of urine, found in the entrails of sacrificed animals and men.

Urini The oracular way by which the will of the god was ascertained.

I once saw a scientific program on television where a surgeon, holding a kidney ready to be transplanted, demonstrated that he could tell it was in good health because when he pressed it with his finger it expelled urine of the right colour. The surgeon believed the organ would save another man's life. In ancient times, the Roman *haruspices* believed that the omens they found in the entrails of sacrificed animals could save their entire tribe.

Returning to our examination of the Orique Fields, we see that this place of oracular rituals was also used by the Jewish community. The Jews had a religious ceremony where they killed a man on the cross as a scapegoat, for the salvation of the whole tribe. During the Purim festival, they took omens from the dying king, either by drams, by urim (an artefact inserted into the high priest's breastplate), or by prophets.

Parallel to Sun Street there is a street called Arrábida, which is related to a Jewish word for safety. A long time ago, the Jews who settled along the river Sado, in the city of Setúbal, Portugal, called the hills nearby Arrábida, the sacred and safe place. These settlers belonged to a sect called the Sadducees.

Sadducees

The Sadducees were one of the four principal Jewish sects. Their founder, Zadok, was a rabbi who lived about a thousand years before Jesus. The doctrines of his master, Antigonus, were that we should practice virtue neither in the hope of a reward nor fear of punishment in another life, but solely because of its intrinsic excellence. The Sadducees, then, denied both resurrection and the immortality of the soul, and disbelieved in angels and spirits. Though reproaching them for misunderstanding the scriptures, Jesus did not censure them for their morals, which as a result have been (on doubtful grounds) considered strict. The Sadducees attained the highest dignities and offices, even of the priesthood.

Seven: A mystical number

Pythagoras called seven the number of religion. My father tells me that one saying of his grandfather's was "the woman has the craft of seven foxes." There are seven lower heavens: those of Jupiter, Mars, Mercury, the moon, Saturn, the sun, and Venus. There were seven wonders of the ancient world. There are seven days in a week. In Greek, Celtic, Japanese, and Australian aboriginal[1] lore there are seven magnificent people.

According to tradition, sevens saturated the holy place where my father was born. There were seven rivers nearby, and the seven windmills of the Casal Ventoso still bear witness to the sacred mysticism of that place. These mills were probably invented by the Celts, but Greek mythology credits them to Myles or Mylantes. They were moved by the labour of slaves, criminals, or asses. Water mills seem to have been a later invention, used by the Romans from the time of Augustus.

The oracular mysteries concerned a mysterious, ancient cult, involving extraordinary revelations that sought to solve the mysteries of existence through the contemplation of ideas beyond human comprehension. The character and events of the oracles' dramatic performance, which were purposefully designed to perplex, were drawn from sacred enigmatic rites and ceremonies known and practiced only by the initiated. There were also seven magical words, and by saying the correct formula seven times into a person's ear, they could be made to sink to their knees.

---

[1] "The Story of the Seven Sisters and the Faithful Lovers," accessed 27 June 2016, http://www.sacred-texts.com/aus/mla/mla03.htm.

Rua do arco carvalhao: Street of the arch of the oak

Since this was the magical, oracular place, we should expect to find a sacred oak tree there. As we know, under a huge oak the omens were read and the auguries interpreted. For that reason, we can find a clue to its location in the surviving place of the sacred giant oak, now transformed into a street.

According to Greek mythology, the oracle of Dodona was the most ancient in Greece. Some classical authors tell us the huge oak was forty metres high and that its branches extended for fifty metres. The oracle belonged to Zeus, and near its splendid temple was a sacred grove where there was a prophetic oak.

The priestesses announced divine communications in different ways. They approached the holy tree and listened to the rustling of its leaves, or standing by the fountain at its foot, they observed the murmuring of the water that gushed forth. They also prophesied from the sounds that came from brazen vessels suspended from the tree.

Meia laranja: Half an orange

In Celtic and Greek myth, the daughters of Hesperus, who were possessors of the golden fruit, the *Hesperidium*, were watched over by a dragon at the western ends of the earth. Half an orange was part of the ritual of the dying king.

Every year, twelve days after Carnival or *Mardi Gras*, on the third day of the full moon, the Druids—priests of the pagan church—chose by lots the king who was to die on the cross as a scapegoat for the salvation of the tribe. These lots were organised in a basket full of ribbons, which was hung on the sacred oak tree.

The participants in the ritual would form a circle under the tree, and one of the couples would hold the end of a ribbon. On the command of one of the priests, they would pull down the ribbons, and the pair whose ribbon was attached to a pine cone would be elected king and queen of the next *Mardi Gras*. The recreation of this ritual, now without the crucifixion, still occurs today in Portugal, and even in Australia at the Portuguese clubs.

In Lisbon the name of this ritual survives, in the name "A Rua do Arco Carvalhao, na Meia Laranja." Why half an orange? Sometimes half an orange is used instead of the pine cone; and it is possible to use a cake to choose the king by lot, as the Romans and Celts did. During Saturnalia, which developed into our Carnival, the Romans would bake a cake, the King's Cake, with a broad bean inside. Then the candidates were served a slice of cake. The person who received a gift in his slice walked away free. But the one who got the bean was elected the king of Saturnalia, and would live like a king for a year before being sacrificed at the next Saturnalia on the third day of the full moon, with his death considered a scapegoat for the salvation of the tribe. The Celts used a similar ritual during the Beltane festival.

Today in Portugal, the King's Cake is a delicacy essential to any Portuguese table during Christmas and King's Day, twelve days after Christmas. And in Portugal, as we have noted, there is still the old saying, "*Rei morto, rei posto*" (Dead king, elected king). Just as in ancient times, the King's Cake is still baked with a gift and the broad bean. But the one who gets the bean no longer has to pay with his life; instead he must only buy the cake the following year. The one who gets the gift still represents the other scapegoat who would walk free, just as in the original ritual. In modern times, the gift is generally hidden for the children to find; the parents leave it for them as something to get excited about, and this excitement is symbolic of the joy of walking away freely.

Dionysus and the cemetery of pleasures

My father tells me that during his childhood, he habitually played in a graveyard called "The cemetery of pleasures", but now he asks why a cemetery should have such a name. Perhaps it is because until we experience death, we cannot say whether those who have experienced the afterlife may experience more pleasure than we do. Or perhaps the answer is to be found in the festivals of Dionysus.

The feasts consecrated to Bacchus or Dionysus, the god of wine, came from thanksgiving festivals that the ancients solemnised after the vintage. According to Greek mythology, Bacchus invented the preparation of a beverage from grapes in the vales of Nysa, and taught the making of wine. To spread the knowledge of his invention, he travelled almost the whole known world, and received divine honours everywhere. He rewarded those who received him hospitably and worshipped him. Several people shared his love, but Ariadne was elevated to the position of his wife, and shared his immortality. To confer the same favour on his mother, Semele, he descended into the underworld realms of Pluto and conducted her to Olympus.

256

In the dreadful war with the giants, Dionysus fought heroically and saved the gods from impending ruin. During the rejoicing at the gods' victory, Zeus joyfully cried out to him, "*Evan evoe*" ("well done, my son"), and he was usually saluted with these words thereafter.

We often find Dionysus represented with the round, soft and graceful form of a maiden, rather than that of a young man, and the tiara is an ornament peculiar to him. His long, wavy hair is held behind his head in a knot, and wreathed with sprigs of ivy and vine leaves. Usually he is naked, though sometimes he has an ample mantle hung negligently around his shoulders, and at other times a fawn skin hangs across his breast. The bearded Bacchus is probably of Indian or Egyptian origin.

The feasts consecrated to Bacchus or Dionysus were in Latin called *Bacchanalia* (Portuguese: *bacanal* or *bacchanal*), and in Greek *Dionysia* or more generally *orgia* (orgies). The great Dionysian festivals were celebrated in spring, and the most important part of the celebration was the procession representing the god's triumph. This involved bacchants and bacchantes who, inspired by real or feigned intoxication, wandered about rioting and dancing, and gave themselves to the most extravagant licentiousness. They were masked and clothed in fawn skins and crowned with ivy. The female initiates worshipped the phallus and underwent ritual whipping. In Portugal today, when a woman loses her virginity, they say "*Ela perdeu os tres vintens*" ("she lost her third vintage").

From the thanksgiving rituals in honour of joy, with wild songs and comic dances, came the drama and songs of the chorus (the *fados*) that accompanied the sacrifice of the goat, which became more popular over time. The *fado*, including the speaking *fado*, the *falado*, and the chorus alternated the praises of Bacchus with moral reflections as the narration required. The singers' reward, if they satisfied the audience, was a goat.

Sporting dances were also introduced, mingled with pranks and everything that excited laughter. These went with the *fado no gozo*, songs of pleasure or enjoyment. The original ritual that had developed from the killing of kings was performed at the crossways and later in villages on moveable stages. These stories were sometimes serious and had solemn choruses, while at other times they were comic and accompanied by dances. Such representations were called tragedies—songs of the sacrifice of the goat—or songs of the vintage, which included comedies, festive dances, and satirical actions (*drama satyricum*). These sports were finally exhibited with much more splendour on the stages of the towns, and acquired a more distinct character, with a particular tone and morality.

The Dionysian feasts passed from the Greeks to the Romans, who celebrated them with even greater dissoluteness as Bacchanalia in the cemeteries, until the Senate abolished them in 187 BC. But despite their persecution, the orgies or bacchanals have survived until today, all over the world.

In Portugal, the *bacanal* and *orgia* have survived in the physical place of the cult (*O Cemiterio dos Prazeres*). But above all, they have survived through their beautiful and historical poetic aspect. The *fado*, our national folk song, with all its dramatic elements, has also survived in the forms of the *fado falado* and the less popular *fado dançado*.

Casal ventoso post quam (altos ventum) in
montes atque invia lustra

Lustral Related to purification from guilt or appeasement of the gods; belonging to a period of five years; quinquennial.

Lustral sacrificium A sacrifice of purification; an offering of appeasement.

Lustrum A purification, sacrifice, after completing the census, in which a swine, a sheep and a bull were offered.

Suovetaurilia, exercitium omnem suovetaurilibus luvit

Suovetaurilia is a classic example of a religious festival common to the most important games of ancient Europe. This ritual took place according to a quinquennial period and involved a triad sacrifice that took place in the high mountains overlooking the seaside, a place of strong winds. These winds are the reason for the seven mystical windmills of the Casal Ventoso (Village of the Wind).

20. Ancient combat sports

by Ivo Rato

Combat sports such as *pankration* were an essential feature of the Ancient Olympics, and retain a significant place in the modern games. But their study requires a more professional approach than is usually taken at present. To be a top university professor, or even a member of the International Olympic Committee (IOS) is not enough to provide an appropriate understanding of what was the most important sport of the ancient festival.

The art of self-defence

Unlike many animals, man has not received from nature any appendages that particularly useful as weapons. He must use artificial means to increase his strength when he attacks, and to shield his unprotected body. As a result, arms were among the earliest inventions, and were perhaps in the first instance used to defend against animals. But they were soon also used in conflict between men.

The first and most natural of all weapons were the club and the sling. The Greek hero Heracles, the Gaulish Ogmios, and the Irish Ogma are all described as wielding clubs, while the Bible tells us that David killed Goliath with a slingshot. The slingshot was also the first weapon the children on street learned to make, out of a V-shaped branch, two rubber bands, and a piece of leather. So armed, we managed to attack the territories of the kids on nearby streets. We used little rocks as ammunition, with the sling adding force to the cast.

These little street wars sometimes took on a more alarming, martial aspect. Very often, forces from different streets met on the borders of each territory and resumed the street quarrels in single combat, conducted in the following manner. A committee of members from each side scratched a line in the ground and then brought the champions of each street forward. Then the fighters had to agree on the type of fighting to be engaged in, be it only punching or "*a vale tudo menos tirar olhos*" ("anything goes except taking the eyes").

After the contenders had agreed on the rules, the challenge started. The fighters spat over the line, into the opponent's territory, and then each quickly stood on the spit with his right foot. After doing that, they accepted the challenge by sweeping over the spit with their foot.

The Portuguese expression *Vale tudor,* meaning *anything goes*, is now in fashion in many martial-arts schools, especially in the United States and Australia, thanks to the Brazilian Garcia family, who developed a form of no-holds-barred combat based on the ancient rules of *pankration* (Portuguese: *pancracio*).

The rise of pankration

Pankration was the ancients' attempt to combine self-defence with poetry. As long as courage, strength, and dexterity decided the outcome of a battle, war held great appeal for noble-minded people. In the history of military confrontation, we must give single combat a special place. Among the Celts, Greeks, and Romans, the outcome of a battle was often decided in single combat between the champions of both armies. The film *Troy* (2004) gives us a perfect representation of such single combat, under which the art of self-defence attained a high degree of perfection.

In this period, science was also becoming incorporated into society. By the strong bones of the skull, nature has protected man against a downward blow far more than against a thrust, to which the more vulnerable breast and belly are exposed. So great is the difference between the head and the torso, in this respect, that a downward blow with the fist hardly ever causes serious injury, but the thrusting blows of a boxer or kick-boxer are highly dangerous.

As they better understood human anatomy, men developed fighting techniques to be used mainly against each other. Nature has given us only two weapons, and in a very limited sense of the word—the arm and the leg. These can truly be made weapons only by the dexterity acquired through long training. As their understanding progressed, the Celts and Greeks developed the art called *pankration* or *pancracio*. Its name makes it literally the art of universal power: *pan* means *universal* and *kratos* means *power*.

Cato pancracio is the equivalent of *O vale tudo*, the no-holds-barred fight. In *pankration* men enter a close struggle where they may grab each other and often fall to the ground. In this circumstance, many techniques of boxing and kickboxing lose their effect, so the ancients strove continually to invent techniques that could also be used on the ground. Through their progress in this direction, they developed the *cato pancracio*, which mixes kickboxing and wrestling.

Pankration and the myth of Asian martial arts

There is a common belief among modern martial artists that self-defence techniques such as the arts of karate, kung fu, taekwondo, judo, aikido, Viet Vo Dao, Muay Thai, and many other styles, along with modern kickboxing, all originated in Asia. But most of the techniques used in Asian martial arts were in reality well-developed by Europeans by the time of the ancient games of Europe.

At the Nemean Games of 400 BC, for example, Damoxenus of Syracuse attacked Creugas of Epidammus with an open hand to the stomach, ripping out his entrails and causing a swift death. Creugas was posthumously crowned with the garland of victory since in the Greek sacred games athletes were not allowed to kill and Damoxenus had therefore to be disqualified.

Spearhand (*nukite*) is a Japanese karate technique also used in other styles of martial arts. It teaches how to attack the soft parts of one's opponent's body with a strike of the middle three fingers. The front kick called *gastrizen* by the Greeks is equivalent to the karate technique called *mai-geri*. A judo technique

264

involving sacrifice, the stomach throw called *tomoe nage* in Japanese, was one of the favourite techniques of the pancratists in the Ancient Olympics. In antiquity, this move caused spectators to roar with excitement, and it has the same effect at the modern Olympics. In the *tomoe nage*, the athlete sacrifices his position and falls down on his back to pull his opponent over the top of him and send him flying headfirst through the air.

Martial arts in ancient Rome

The school at Capua was one of the most famous of those that trained gladiators for the Colosseum. One of the things they taught their students was that the typical gladiator, when they went down on their back for a throw, typically fell too far from their opponent and was not sufficiently beneath them for the move to have maximum effect. Another fault the trainers of Capua noticed, which occurs very often, was that the throwing leg was kept too straight at the beginning of a throw. Actually, the balancing leg should be well bent until the throw is complete, and should only be straightened afterward.

Curiously, after intensive research into the ancient combat sports, I realised that what I had learned from my teacher Master Kobayashi, thirty years ago, included techniques that were familiar to Europeans more than two thousand years ago. We should be grateful to the people of Asia for preserving these ancient techniques of self-defence. However, because of widespread ignorance about the origins of these martial arts, the law in some countries goes to the ridiculous extent of forbidding its citizens from teaching martial arts unless they join oriental associations.

The Portuguese, many of whom are descendants of the Lusitanos, were intellectually colonised by Christianity well over a thousand years ago. More recently, since 1960, youth interested in physical cultivation have been dominated by the modern religion of oriental martial arts. I have been a victim of both dogmas—both Catholicism and this oriental myth. Thanks to the archaic coalition between the Church and a dictatorship lasting nearly fifty years, my people grew up in comparative intellectual darkness, especially where the culture of our ancestors was concerned. I also fell victim to the myth of martial arts' oriental origin, being flatly forbidden by Portugal's Martial Arts Board to teach in my own country, for the simple reason that I refused to join a Japanese association.

Australia: The country of Celtic martial arts

Thousands of years ago, the Celts introduced their martial arts to places all along the silk route, as far as China. When I came to Australia, I joined the most powerful martial-arts organisation in the country—the Red Dragon, guided by one of the world's most charismatic instructors, the Celtic chieftain Bob Jones.

Even those who do not practice the art of self-defence will be aware of the proliferation of martial-arts schools in the West. Thanks to a high standard of living and close proximity to Asia, Australia is a place of pilgrimage for masters of all kinds of martial arts, who come looking for a sort of El Dorado. This gives Australians an incredible opportunity to analyse the panorama of the arts of self-defence, to consider an almost unlimited variety of styles, and for everyone who is interested in this mystical subject to choose the path that appeals to them most.

I must pay homage here to my teacher and friend Bob Victor Jones, whose middle name comes from the Latin *vinco* or *victum*, meaning to conquer, or one who conquers in war. His parents, who are of Welsh descent on his mother's side and Irish descent on his father's, gave Bob this name. Nothing happens without a reason, and he not only conquered martial-arts competitions in Australia and New Zealand, but also won the hearts of people of the many nationalities that make up the Australian population. I was no exception, and chose the Red Dragon school as the place to undertake my training.

When war broke out in East Timor in 1975, I went to Darwin, where I joined the Red Cross. After spending some time in the camps there, helping refugees, I went back to Portugal. Armed with the black belt I had attained at the Red Dragon school, I decided to open a martial-arts school of my own, but was forbidden to teach because I refused to join one of the Japanese associations in Lisbon. Even as a Portuguese person who had served in the special forces during the colonial war, in peacetime I could not teach martial arts without the authorisation of technocrats under the guidance of a Japanese organisation.

My disappointment with this arbitrary regulation took me to the limits of my patience, especially since I had formed Portugal's first martial arts organisation. Such a nonsensical curtailment of individual rights endangered the sovereignty of the Lusitanians, who had been warriors of the sun. This should perhaps not have been a surprise: Portugal had become used to totalitarian rule where the army holds all power and democracy is forbidden. Despite the democratic revolution of 25 April 1974, a high official in the navy still held a position that allowed them to control the Martial Arts Board.

I found myself facing a complex dilemma, where I felt compelled to fight an abhorrent law, the Japanese associations, and a Portuguese navy commander, all at once. The sad irony of this ordeal was that the marines of the Portuguese navy had, 450 years ago, forever changed the nature of war in Japan by introducing firearms to the country. Now we found a similar shift imposed upon us, as the Japanese associations colluded in the suppression of Portugal's own martial heritage.

Japan

Fernão Mendes Pinto, a navigator and writer, tells in his book *Peregrinação* that on sailing from Malacca and arriving in Japan in 1542, he became the first European to trade goods with the Japanese. Mendes Pinto and two other Portuguese, Francisco Moura and João Morais, went ashore and were confronted by Tanegashima Tokitaka, the local lord.

Moura realised that Tanegashima was very curious about the arquebus, a primitive, muzzle-loaded rifle, and demonstrated using it to shoot down some birds. The Japanese were so impressed that Tanegashima offered to buy Moura's arquebus, and when the Portuguese refused this offer, Moura was invited to stay on the island where they had landed and was offered the lord's daughter as a wife if he agreed to remain and teach the Japanese how to make more guns.

This incident was a great turning point for warfare in Japan. After the introduction of firearms, the art of war was reduced to an impersonal system, and lost most of its charm for the country's nobility, who were at once idle and ambitious. Nevertheless, some were optimistic about the potential of these new weapons, and took advantage of the introduction of the arquebus. One such person was the warlord Oda Nobunaga, who eventually unified much of central Japan, which was then divided into warring fiefdoms, but was only eight years old at the time of Moura's landing on the island of Tanegashima.

In 1568, with the aid of firearms, Oda conquered the city of Kyoto. Then, in 1575, at the Battle of Nagashino, he defeated a great force of mounted samurai and archers with a force including 3,000 arquebusiers. After Oda's death, his successor, Totomi Hideyoshi, also adopted the use of arquebuses in his armies.

So, while Portugal had given rise to modern Japanese warfare in the sixteenth century, in the twentieth I found problems teaching martial arts in Portugal because the Japanese had established a stranglehold over our own martial education. Though the navy had opened the doors of the jails, let out the old political prisoners and refilled the cells with the political police of the fascists, the high-ranking navy officer who led the Martial Arts Board persisted in reinforcing the obsolete law, originating from military headquarters, that allowed the closing of any school not affiliated with the Japanese monopoly.

I was not, of course, the Martial Arts Board's sole opponent. The organisation's aim was to protect the monopoly a few karate styles had over martial-arts education. But the naval commander's zeal in enforcing the regulation was extreme; when a famous 8-dan karate master of the Gôjû-ryû—an organisation that was not on the approved list—arrived from Japan to give a karate seminar in Porto, Portugal's second city, the commander ordered a nearby police station to search the dojo. In the press conference he later gave, the master said he was astonished, and that even the Americans, after the Second World War, had never invaded a Japanese dojo with machine guns.

This was the scenario I found in my own country—after a democratic revolution! But I was a black belt, and you cannot simply buy this belt in a shop—it was my reward for the training I had undergone and the knowledge I had accumulated. I was also the son of a Portuguese sailor who had spent forty-seven years navigating the trade routes first traced by our ancestors. If I had been a good enough soldier to potentially die for my country in war, I was good enough to stand up for my rights, I decided.

If my thoughts were good, my actions were even better. To ridicule the capricious Martial Arts Board and its white-collar members, I challenged the Japanese instructor the government had hired to train the riot police to a kickboxing match. Although the challenge received no reply, it nevertheless altered the state of martial arts in Portugal for the better. Even the Madeira Islands, the Pearl of the Atlantic, where the famous navigator Christopher Columbus had lived with his Portuguese wife, were liberated from the Martial Arts Board.

Madeira is a two-hour flight from the mainland, and at the time, its chief of police was an army major. Any time he received an order from military headquarters, signed by the navy commander, he simply enforced the order. He had no idea that some of these orders were the expression of the personal vendettas of the boss of the Martial Arts Board, and not official documents. After I moved to Madeira and alerted the major to this unlawful situation, he reopened the martial-arts schools previously closed by the police.

I tell this story to introduce two fundamental issues:

1. The martial arts did not originate in the orient, but were also the common practices of the warriors of ancient Europe.

2. In ancient times, combatants were selected more fairly than they are today. Only the best were allowed to compete in the sacred games.

As I write this, I can obviously not be concerned about myself: according to Pindar, the martial contests of the games are not suitable for anyone past their physical prime, and for me this is certainly past. Yet, my heart still bleeds to see the anti-democratic institution of the International Olympic Committee (IOC) rob thousands of athletes who are not part of the Olympic conspiracy of their dreams of competition and possible victory.

The taekwondo knockout

In ancient times, before they could compete in the Olympics, athletes had to submit to a month of hard training in the city of Elis, which was responsible for the Olympic festival. Apart from planning the big event, the main reason for this period of preparation was to ensure that only the best athletes competed at the games. In fact, many never made it to Olympia because they did not reach the Olympic standards. Today, in the modern Olympics, each country's national Olympic Committee administers the ancient rule of the city of Elis. As we know, each country selects its best athletes and sends them to the Olympic host country in the hope of winning the coveted medals.

Taekwondo appeared at the Olympics for the first time as a demonstration sport at the 1988 summer games, which were held in Seoul, the Korean capital. According to tradition, the Greeks also had demonstration sports at the Ancient Olympic Games, perhaps to gauge the public reaction before adding a new event to the festival. Since Taekwondo is Korea's national sport, it was only natural that the Koreans, who had spent so much money on hosting the games—as is necessary of host countries these days—should attempt to promote it. I thought it a good omen, since the introduction of one style of martial arts seemed as though it could open the way for freestyle competition and finally millions of martial artists would have the chance to compete for their countries.

The inclusion of freestyle martial arts in the Olympics would have been a great historical achievement. But it was not to be.

Pankration and the modern Olympics

I have mentioned *pankration* before in discussing the combat sports of the ancients. It is "the sport of all strength", and was, for more than a thousand years, the most important event of the original Olympic Games. But in the final years of the nineteenth century, when Baron de Coubertin started the modern Olympic movement, it was not introduced along with other combat sports such as boxing and wrestling—possibly because it was entirely unknown to the organisers.

There were two types of *pankration* in ancient Europe, the *pancracio*, which is similar to freestyle fighting, and the *cato pancracio*, which is similar to the modern *val tudo*, or no-holds-barred fight.

With the advent of taekwondo at the 1988 Olympics, it appeared as though a revival of *pankration*, absent since the last Olympics in 395 AD, would finally return in the form of a freestyle martial-arts competition. But in its eagerness to create a monopoly for financial gain, one Korean organisation colluded with the IOC to decide that there would be no freestyle competition at the Olympics and that only one style from the many around the world would be admitted—taekwondo.

This was only the beginning of the unsporting behaviour seen from the Korean taekwondo promoters and the IOC. In an avaricious manner, they even knocked out rival taekwondo associations from the competition, denying the right to represent their country to athletes who were not paying members of the appropriate organisation. Seeing this, one must ask—are the modern Olympics a humanitarian, fraternal, and peace-promoting international event? And is one's choice of style crucial to the final victory in a fight?

Martial arts are not a dance. They have grace and beauty, but dance is for joy while combat is for survival. Yes, the two have many elements in common: they both need hard work, dexterity, a good sense of balance, concentration, dedication, and personal ability. The late Bruce Lee was a good dancer, as have been many other famous movie stars, including Jean-Claude Van Damme, also a martial artist, and Patrick Swayze.

In 1975, while training for my black belt at the Zen Do Kai headquarters in Elizabeth Street, Melbourne, I was also teaching ballroom dancing at the Arthur Murray School, one of the most famous ballroom schools in the world, which was just across the road. In ballroom competitions, the pairs on the dance floor are often highly skilled, so in the compulsory steps of the different rhythms, the judges make their selection based on the couples' grace and beauty. What school they come from is irrelevant. It is not the style of the school, but the excellence in the individual performance that makes for victory. Similarly, in freestyle combat, there is no specific style required, and the judges award the victory to the most effective fighter.

The taekwondo monopoly

Who was behind the absurd martial-arts monopoly we now have in the modern Olympics? If we consult the Yellow Pages in any country, we can see that no other sport has so many schools as do the martial arts. If there are so many schools, it can only be because they exist to serve the demand of millions of adepts of these mystical arts.

No other sport can put so many practitioners together as can the martial arts. But the Olympic movement, while proclaimed humanitarian, fraternal, and peace-promoting motives, has decided to exclude millions of martial-arts practitioners from the games and permit only one style: taekwondo. This attitude alone is a kick in the face to thousands of athletes around the world, and a cruel rejection of their work. Yet, the swindlers of the IOC went even further, giving the monopoly to only one of multiple taekwondo associations.

I am not against taekwondo. Quite the contrary. For more than a thousand years, the combat sports were the most famous events of the Ancient Olympics, and so I believe that as a martial sport, taekwondo should have been part of the Olympics a long time ago—along with every one of the world's other martial-arts styles.

What is a style?

Every martial-arts school claims that its style is superior to all others. I believe some styles *are* better than others, but a style is also a collection of techniques aimed at a goal common to all martial-arts schools: victory in combat. It is in combat that we see the style is only expressed through the student: no matter how good the style is, if you do not dedicate yourself to the art, you will never achieve anything with it. Selecting the correct style is not what makes you a champion.

So, the different styles are different ways up the mountain. If you are persistent, you will reach the top; it doesn't matter which way you walk. A beautiful style can enable the one who performs with graceful technique to defeat their opponent with a knockout, but in a kickboxing fight, the combatants avoid displaying these beautiful techniques. It is true that at any moment they might pull off a spectacular high leg technique and cause the audience to cheer with joy, but many fighters prefer not to show off in this way, sacrificing beauty for efficiency.

Many times, spectacular techniques win over the public but cost a fighter the final victory. Suppose A is kicking B with the most beautiful and acrobatic technique. The crowd is on its feet, applauding in a frenzy. But suddenly, B blocks his opponent's leg and hits him with an ugly fist to the chin, knocking him out and sending him straight to the canvas. B has sacrificed beauty and waited for the right moment to make an effective strike, and in return he has earned the victory. This is just one example that shows how style is not an essential component of victory in the martial arts. In a more philosophical way, we could say that styles do not pre-exist the fight, but develop at the right moment according to the situation.

The avaricious attitude of the IOC, in presuming to make just one style stand for all of the martial arts, sets a dangerous example in a context where good leadership is essential. The original games took place under the guidance of Zeus, the chief judge, who lived on Mount Olympus with the other gods who presided over the games. He was the wisest of gods, the giver of good advice, and a true witness. His promises were irrevocable and infallible. He knew the fates of men, heard the oaths of mortals who sword by his name, and punished perjury against such oaths severely. All injustice and cruelty were hateful to him, and so if anyone was caught cheating in the games, they would be disqualified and had to offer a statue to Zeus, which was called a Zane:

> According to Pausanias (V, 21, 2–18), the first of the Zanes were erected after the ninety-eighth Olympiad in 388 BC, when Eupolos from Thessaly was fined for bribing three of his opponents in the boxing event. The remaining six statues were erected after the 112th Olympiad in 332 BC by the Athenian Kallipos, an athlete of the pankration who also bribed his opponents. Pausanias mentions in detail other similar stories, ending with that of Sarapion from Alexandria, an athlete of the pankration, who fled on the eve of the contest in the 201st Olympiad, in AD 25. He is the only Olympic athlete to have been punished for cowardice.[1]

Today, there is no one capable of punishing Olympic bureaucrats for their unfairness—no Zeus appears to be watching over them. So this new millennium seems likely to have the

---

[1]Olympia Vickatou, "Zanes," *Odysseys*, accessed 27 June 2016, http://odysseus.culture.gr/h/2/eh251.jsp?obj_id=5824.

dollar continuing to run faster than tradition, and to see the insolent and the expedient triumph over the sacred rule that the victory should go to the most excellent athletes in the land.

The Olympic police

These days, it costs billions of dollars to host the Olympics. The 2000 games in Sydney were no exception, and the entire Australian population sacrificed greatly to stage the games. When modern sporting facilities are built with taxpayers' money, it means that other public spending is foregone. It is, then, outrageously unfair for there to be Olympic rules that deny young champions the chance to represent their country.

Let's imagine there is a seventeen-year-old Australian called Young Freeman. He goes to high school and has a part-time job that supports his participation in his favourite sport, taekwondo. He has been training for ten years by now, and has attained a very high level of skill. He is physically and mentally strong, and believes he is the ideal person to represent his country in this sport.

But to his surprise, Young Freeman realises that the school where he has trained for the past ten years does not participate in the Olympic conspiracy. So our champion, who as a taxpayer has contributed to the building of Olympic facilities in his country, cannot represent that country in his chosen sport, in spite of his superior ability.

Bob Jones, my martial-arts instructor, has 25,000 students in Australia alone, including some of the world's best fighters. Yet, not one of them could compete in the Sydney Olympics on behalf of their country of origin because they did not begin to the right Korean organisation. Interestingly, Jones's students could have tried out for any other competition under the Olympic banner, but in the martial arts, they were definitively excluded.

21. Lessons from history

Those who believe history is only a thing of the past should think again. History always repeats itself.

Annibal Barca and Operation Desert Storm

It doesn't take a hero to order men into battle, but it takes a hero to lead from the front. General H. Norman Schwarzkopf, the commander of Operation Desert Storm, won the affection of his fellow Americans with a style of leadership that was more demanding—and more trusting—than that of any other American leader since Eisenhower.

On 27 February 1991, the war against Iraq was over. The Americans and their allies had accomplished their objectives with minimal casualties and in record time. During the campaign, General Schwarzkopf used tactics employed by Annibal Barca at the Battle of Cannae in 216 BC—a classic double-envelopment manoeuvre that can allow an inferior force to defeat a superior one on open terrain. At Cannae, on Italy's east coast, in two days the Roman army lost some of their best generals and around 80,000 soldiers to the Carthaginians. The Carthaginian general and his Celtic allies, on the other hand, lost only around 6,000 warriors. The same tactics worked for Schwarzkopf and the Americans in Iraq: we can see that history repeats itself.

If this principle, that history repeats, applies in war, then surely it can also apply in peace.

Babylonia, Baghdad, and the Olympics

I will race the Chariot of Knowledge in the streets of Baghdad, trying to spread peace. It is not my intention to race for the laurel garland of the Nobel Peace Prize. But since we are talking about history, let's analyse the past to find the secrets of peace.

We have learned that at the time of the Ancient Olympics, all the city-states of Greece had to respect the sacred truce that was in place because of the games. In this book, the Chariot of Knowledge, we have learned that the games were held in accordance with traditions from the biblical scriptures of the Old Testament, and we have seen the meaning behind the strict imposition of the sacred truth. We have also found the important fact that the Hebrew scribes borrowed extensively from earlier traditions when composing their scriptures, and particularly from *The Epic of Gilgamesh*. In fact, the rabbis even brought the Hebrew alphabet from Babylonia, where it had its remote origins in the Sumerian cuneiform writing going back as far as 3,300 BC.

The Sumerians invented writing and literature, including much of the Western world's religious mythology. These are our spiritual ancestors, who created the Bible and generated the peace that inspired the sacred truce of the Ancient Olympics. But in our day, their descendants live in the world's most turbulent region.

Living in peace with one's neighbours

The Spanish and Portuguese fought each other for centuries, but today they are like brothers. As a Portuguese citizen, I can choose to live in Spain at any time. The people have not changed; they are pretty much the same as they ever were. But the political climate has changed. Could Jews and Arabs ever live together in peace? The example of the Portuguese and the Spanish offers great hope.

Let's analyse the history of the Arabs and the Jews. They are both Semitic peoples, said to be descended from Shem (*Genesis 10*). In fact, linguistics tells us that both Arabic and Hebrew are Semitic languages, as are Aramaic, the language of the Talmud, and Assyrian and Babylonian.

The golden age of ancient Iberia, the Spanish Babylonia

After the Moorish invasion of 711 AD, the Iberian Peninsula became the most advanced place on earth, thanks to a tolerant, multicultural environment that respected and protected multiple religions. The Sephardim (Jews from the Iberian Peninsula) worked with Arab scholars to prepare the way for the European Renaissance. Paper was manufactured for the first time, and immense libraries were opened to the public. Córdoba had the largest library in Europe, with more than a million books. Algebra was invented. Christians adopted Moorish habits and became known as Mozarabs. Even the famous Jewish scholar and doctor Hasdai ibn Shaprut became the personal physician of the Caliph of Córdoba, which shows remarkable trust between the Arabs and Jews of the time. This peaceful environment facilitated commerce with other parts of the world, and brought great prosperity to the region, and Christians from other parts of Europe migrated to Iberia.

Because history always repeats itself, Portuguese is today one of the most spoken languages in France after French, and Paris is the second-largest "Portuguese city", based on its some 700,000 Portuguese inhabitants.[1] From their Gallic origins, some Portuguese have returned to their starting point.

Moors and Christians lived and worked together in the tolerant Iberian society until the rise of the Catholic Inquisition. Then the Iberian Peninsula went into a cultural decline that has only recently begun to reverse.

In Australia, different religions and cultures used to live in peace. Today we struggle to do the same; as in the past, the Inquisition or religion can destroy societies. In this, my beloved Celtic country, we have the world's most tolerant society. It is the closest place I can think of to paradise, and we don't need a holy war.

---

[1] Wikipedia contributors, "Languages of France," *Wikipedia, The Free Encyclopedia*, accessed 27 June 2016, https://en.wikipedia.org/w/index.php?title=Languages_of_France&oldid=724439390; Manel Oliveira, 18 February 2014, response to "What Are Some Mind-blowing Facts about Portugal," *Quora*, accessed 27 June 2016, https://www.quora.com/What-are-some-mind-blowing-facts-about-Portugal.

22. Atlantis

The phrase "afraid the sky might fall on our heads" was a saying of the ancient Celts, suggesting an imminent and spectacular catastrophe. We believe this remarkable phrase is probably related to the cataclysm that destroyed Atlantis, and that the Celts were a branch of its survivors' descendants. The idea of the sky falling on our heads references a fear of great disaster that has been passed from generation to generation. It feels as though it could describe a volcanic eruption. And it is reasonable to suggest that the Atlanteans, because of the loss of their homeland in such a dramatic way, decided never again to build a city. Through these fragments of evidence, we can see a way to rethink the possible origins of the Celts.

Atland eller Manhein, a work in Latin and Swedish by O. Rudbeck, the first volume of which appeared in 1675, tries to prove the hypothesis that Sweden was the Atlantis of the ancients, and that the Romans, Greeks, English, Danes, and Germans all had this one origin—suggesting a connection between the various Celtic tribes.

Celtic awareness

Whether it is coincidence or fate, the new millennium belongs to the astrological sign of Aquarius, the water. Some may think that my father is only dreaming if he talks about a rising Celtic awareness, but the European Union has finally taken an interest in quality of life and recently decided to take drastic measures on environmental issues, signifying a revival of the Celtic reverence for nature. The 4th Inter-Celtic Colloquium on Hydrology was held in 2005 in Portugal, the same country where six years earlier my father had been deprived by the leaders of the University of Lisbon of the opportunity to teach Celtic culture to Portuguese students.

The legacy of Atlantis

Portugal and Spain strongly maintain the sacred ritual of bull-fighting, which according to Plato was the greatest festival of Atlantis, staged every five years—on the same sacred quinquennial cycle as the Ancient Olympics. The Iberian Peninsula is also the only place that still organises the running of the bulls, and Portugal is the only country where the *forcados* (bull catchers) still chase the bull barehanded and wrestle it to a stop.

The Iberian Peninsula is the only place where we can see these ancient rituals of Atlantis. These correspond with the descriptions of Plato, who also tells us that Atlantean architects used red, black, and white marble on their building projects—an observation in which we find a remarkable coincidence when we watch the running of the bulls. The Basques of Pamplona, and the Portuguese, still wear white and red garments to harmonise with the black bull. Richard King, our Celtic Druid friend, informs us that these three colours—red, white, and black—are also sacred to the Celts.

These days, intense criticism is often directed at those who

284

are still involved in bullfighting, and especially at the matador, who kills the bull by thrusting a sword between its shoulders, severing the aorta. This is a cruel blow, but it also brings honour to those who have the privilege of delivering it. Because of his strong affinity with remote rituals, the matador is given high respect by those still connected with the ancient traditions. For others, the bullfights are unacceptable, and there is a movement in the Iberian Peninsula to abolish the bullfighting.

I have already expressed my personal ideas about this ancient ritual, which seems likely to be a remembrance of the time of Atlantis. Put in contrast with the acts of cruelty perpetrated around the globe in the name of supposedly high ideals, the sacred bullfight, which venerates the strength and dignity of the sacrificed animal and is rooted in more than 10,000 years of history and mythology, seems rather more humane. Surely, if there is cruelty to be ended, it is in the building of weapons of mass destruction, the way we allow millions of people to die of starvation, and so on.

Animal rights are important, it is true. But the moralists who seek to end the bullfight, most of which are fervent Catholics, should be far more concerned with the suffering of the innocent children victimised by the "sacred" paedophilia of many priests.

In the bullfight or the running of the bulls, any human injured is always an adult. To participate in any activity related to bullfighting, a man must be over eighteen. This contrasts with the paedophile rituals of the Church, where the victims have no age limit—even young boys can be speared by the adult male priest, the bull of heaven.

The law targets the bosses of illegal brothels; they are put in jail and their premises are closed down. When, then, do the moralists opposed to bullfighting activities not join forces to arrest the priests that molest innocent children, and petition the government to close down the churches where such aberrations have occurred?

The immaterialist Celts

Because the Celts did not build great temples of stone like their contemporaries, the Greeks and Romans, historians have often considered them barbarians. But this disregards the Celts' motivations—they built no temples because they rejected materialism. To the Celts, what was important was the spirit: the immaterial soul.

In philosophy, materialism is the ancient view of nature that dominated most ancient Greek thought, poetry, and mythology, however surrounded it may have been by the grace and poetic spirit of the Greek imagination. In decided opposition to the materialist orientation is the Celtic belief in the liberty of man, which is annihilated by a materialistic determinism that denies free will.

So, the ancient Celts had the technology to build temples, but decided not to. And we may well ask—why would we need temples to worship in when there are trees, rivers, and the sun? So thought the Celts. and history has shown that as soon as we began to build temples, we lost our freedom and became slaves to the material world.

Atlantis: The celebrated city

The legend of Atlantis has spread the light of intellectual cultivation through folklore for thousands of years, right down to our own time. Among the ancients, it was the name of an island in the Atlantic, of which Plato gives the first accounts. According to that famous philosopher, Atlantis was one of the first great places of commerce, and established the world's first and finest civilisation. The surrounding coastal area was covered with magnificent and splendid buildings, of which the greatest was the temple of Poseidon. Built of white, red, and black marble, and richly decorated with gold and precious stones, inside it held a statue of Poseidon riding a chariot pulled by dolphins, which was considered the first wonder of the world.

The primordial civilisation of Atlantis was formed from a stock of beautiful and free people, whose motherland unfortunately vanished forever, probably as the result of violent volcanic activity.

Plato's descriptions of where Atlantis was located were vague at best, and placed it at a spot where no island could be found. Most supposed that it had sunk or was destroyed. Some said the Portuguese islands of the Azores, located about 1500km west of the Portuguese coast, are the mountaintops of sunken Atlantis. Fairy tale or coincidence, the people who live in the archipelago of the Azores are still, up to the present day, concerned by the constant volcanic and seismic activity.

23. The modern Olympics

Despite a few scandals and corruption among some IOC officials, the modern Olympics still show us the extraordinary things that human talent can achieve. Unfortunately, the success of the modern Olympics is still the product of some historical ignorance on the part of their founder, Pierre de Coubertin, and also on the part of the French media.

At the end of the nineteenth century, during his campaign to convince the French people to rally behind him to receive the Olympics, the French media accused de Coubertin of anti-patriotism because he wanted to revive the Greek games rather than the French. In the end, de Coubertin won the argument, convincing everyone that it was important to revive the mysticism behind the Greek games.

De Coubertin was lucky that he made his case in the nineteenth century. Today, I would pose him a few simple questions:

- Are you promoting the worship of a god who is a rapist and paedophile?

- Are you trying to revive the Aristotelian philosophy that sees homosexuality as a means of birth control?

- Why don't you revive the Celtic games of Lughnasadh, which celebrate the first harvest?

Through Lughnasadh, I would tell de Coubertin, you would teach the world that water is the source of life and that trees are guardians of water and soil, which unite the heaven and earth. Their roots ensure that rainwater seeps gradually into the earth, and Lughnasadh celebrates the power of fertility in nature. And I would tell him that the Celtic games had more events than the Greek games.

Unfortunately, during the revival of the Ancient Olympics, neither de Coubertin nor the French media researched the games' Celtic background, unlike the emperor Napoleon III, who ordered the lieutenant-colonel Baron de Stoffel to examine the Celtic history of France.

On 4 April 1995, President François Mitterand opened the European Archaeological Centre with the aim of teaching the greatness of the Celtic civilisation. But even this great initiative has not been enough to educate the French people about their wonderful ancestry.

To my pleasant surprise, though, I have found that more than sixty Celtic festivals are now held across Europe. Remarkably, the majority of them are staged in Italy. Evidently, the people of Italy's north know that their ancestors were Celts, and even the city of Rome is staging Celtic festivals.

I am positive that those who read this book will share with me the mystical connection we have with Europe's Celtic heritage, which for many of us is *our* own heritage. Together, we will bring the Celts together once more and

Combine *Europe's Lost Tribal Societies*

www.ingramcontent.com/pod-product-compliance
Lightning Source LLC
Chambersburg PA
CBHW032149080426
42735CB00008B/639